Jesus the Therapist

A man was there who had been sick for thirty-eight years.
Jesus saw him lying there,
and he knew that the man had been sick for such a long
    time;
so he asked him,
"Do you want to be well?"

— John 5:5–6

JESUS THE THERAPIST

Hanna Wolff

Translated by Robert R. Barr

MEYER
STONE
BOOKS

First published as *Jesus als Psychotherapeut:*
Jesu Menschenbehandlung als Modell moderner Psychotherapie,
© 1978 by RADIUS–Verlag GmbH, Stuttgart, West Germany

This English translation is based on the 1985 edition of the German
original. English translation © 1987 by Meyer-Stone Books

Published in the United States by Meyer-Stone Books,
a division of Meyer, Stone, and Company, Inc.,
714 South Humphrey, Oak Park, IL 60304

Cover design: Terry Dugan Design

Manufactured in the United States of America
91 90 89 88 87   5 4 3 2 1

Library of Congress Cataloging in Publication Data
Wolff, Hanna, 1910–

  Jesus the therapist.

  Translation of: Jesus als Psychotherapeut.
  Bibliography: p.
  Includes index.
    1. Jesus Christ — Counseling methods.   I. Title.
  BT590.C78W6513   1987   232.9'04   87-28223
  ISBN 0-940989-11-5
  ISBN 0-940989-10-7 (pbk.)

Contents

Foreword

by John A. Sanford

Psychology is much in vogue today; a trip through any of the
major bookstores will demonstrate the popularity of the subject.
But many of the books that pass for psychology are like the
biblical flowers of the field: they are here for a moment, but
soon fade away. There are many reasons for this. Some of
them appeal to our most egocentric wishes, demands for power,
and childish expectations; such books sell quickly, but soon the
hungry and dissatisfied egos that buy them move on to others
that seem to offer still more. Other books have some substance
to them, but are limited by a materialistic outlook that forces
them to see the psyche in terms of drives and blind instincts.
As a result they lack soul, and have no staying power.

The recent death of a psychologist friend of mine brought
this point home to me. She left me her library in her will,
and it was my task to sort through her books and find a home
for as many of them as I could. I kept a few of them that
I could use myself, and tried to find homes for others. She
was a Jungian analyst, and I readily found people who wanted
the books on Jungian psychology no matter how old they were.
Even books on archetypal motifs that were written in the 1930s
are as alive today as when they were originally written. But a
great many of her books were of the sort you might have read
in the 1950s or 1960s if you had been studying for a Ph.D. in
a university. They were expensive books, carefully prepared,
and representative of the most widely accepted science of that
day, but as far as current reader interest was concerned they

were dead. Not even a used book store to which I took them was interested. Time had passed them by. They had no staying power because they did not speak of the timeless psyche, and were couched in psychological language that is here today and gone tomorrow.

The authors of such books seem to have no religious inclinations, or, if they do, they seem to be able to keep their psychology and religion in separate compartments. It is well known, of course, that psychologies that are based on the prevailing materialistic and rationalistic attitudes of our time are inimical to religion. Behaviorism and Freudian psychology are obvious examples of psychologies that deny the reality of soul and spirit and dismiss humankind's religious inclinations as an aberration and neurosis.

Many people are satisfied with this kind of psychology. If someone goes to a university to study psychology, it is this kind of psychology that will be studied. The spiritual side of human nature is ignored. Well it might be, for if it were observed to be a reality this fact would shatter the philosophical biases on which such a psychology is based.

Others, however, are not able to compartmentalize themselves so easily, nor are they content with the notion that a human being is a product of blind evolution, that personality is a mere epiphenomenon of biological processes, with no spiritual goal in life, and no connection to a divine creative spirit. These people need to bring together a religious understanding with a scientific understanding. They want to understand themselves against the larger background that a religiously oriented understanding alone can provide. For this reason many people who want to understand themselves continue to hold to a religious tradition. Others, forced to abandon their religious traditions because they have become meaningless to them, feel the loss keenly and search for new ways in which to understand the old truths.

Among these people the longing is great but the task is difficult. Where can we find a psychology deep enough and inclusive enough, free enough from collective assumptions, and courageous enough to push beyond the boundaries that confine the thinking of the greater part of humankind today so that the deeper — and higher — elements in human nature can become conscious? And where can we find a religious outlook that is both sublime and practical, and, above all, rooted enough in reality to be grounded in the realities of the human soul? Much of what passes for Christianity today, for instance, makes a mockery of the profound and subtle truths of the New Testament. At its worst, such a "Christian" approach reduces the biblical faith to theologically toned slogans that the "faithful" must espouse and reiterate. Even at its best most Christian theology today is like a potted plant: bland and impotent, it flourishes only in a special container, and its power to grow is limited by its constricted container.

Now and then, however, a psychologist appears whose psychology is not limited by the materialistic hypothesis, and whose religious outlook is not confined by theological strait jackets. Such a psychologist is Hanna Wolff. Because she is open to truth wherever she finds it, her psychology transcends these limitations. It is this quality in her that enables her to see deeply into the person and teaching of Jesus of Nazareth, in whom she sees a physician of the soul, and in whose teachings she sees spiritual and psychological counsel that is as alive today as it was some two thousand years ago. Out of these insights has emerged her book *Jesus the Therapist,* a book in which the "potted plant" that has been made of Christianity is rooted firmly in the soil of the human soul and in living experiences so that it can grow.

Hanna Wolff has a remarkable capacity to move from the broadest and most searching spiritual principles to the most concrete and practical life-applications. She makes Jesus' teaching come alive through the vignettes she provides us of the lives of her patients. What emerges illuminates us both about ourselves and about Jesus. But the Jesus whom we see through the vision that she gives us is no projection of our wishful thinking, no imagined benefactor who will shower us with blessings without making demands, and no fuzzy-minded servant of the childish wishes and wants of our immature egos. To the contrary, she sees in him a person who saw through the façade of people into their deepest hearts, a therapist who relentlessly rooted out that which was not worthy to exist in order that the full divine potential might flourish.

The result is a book that will speak to many people. Certainly it is full of sound insights for therapists. Spiritual directors will also benefit from its biblically-based insights. The parish priest will find in it inspiration for a hundred sermons. The biblical student will discover that it unlocks doors to unsuspected deeper meaning in the Scriptures. But lay people also will benefit, for Jesus spoke to all people and not to any select group, and he addressed himself not to professionals as such but to each of us in our purely human reality.

But why go back to Jesus' teachings at all? Are there not a sufficient number of wise persons today to whom we can listen? One answer is that *Jesus said it better.* His insight is more acute. His teaching method — story and parable — is more searching. His case histories, succinct and practical, are more universally applicable. For when we read *Jesus the Therapist* we cannot avoid the conclusion that Jesus was the first great depth psychologist, and, even to this day, the most unique.

But there is an additional reason why many people will be helped by relating once again to the teachings of Jesus: the need many of us have to reconnect with our religious roots. None of us is an island unto ourselves. All of us have come from a common past which, whether we know it or not, has shaped who we are today and lives on in our unconscious. To simply throw away our religious tradition because it has been made to conform to the spirit of our times and so has lost its power is like cutting off a tree at its base. The ego may think it can disregard its spiritual origins, but the soul hungers for a connection to the original well of water from which she once drank.

This need exists in people of diverse religious faiths. I had occasion a few years ago to lecture on Jungian psychology in Johannesburg. Several black people attended the lecture, and after it was over I made it a point to talk with each one of them. One of them was a woman who was a professional nurse. She welcomed my interest in her and was eager to answer my question, "Why did you come to hear this lecture on Jung?" She told me about her childhood, how she had been raised among

her people, the Xhosa, and had attended a school for African
children run by a Christian Mission. There she had been taught
that the religion of her people was superstition. Later she went
to the university, and there she was taught that religions in general were irrational and meaningless. Her mind tried to accept
all this, but her heart was not satisfied. But somewhere she
had heard that this mysterious Dr. Jung from Switzerland was
different from other psychologists because he placed a value on
religion, so when she heard there was to be a public lecture on
his psychology she came, in the hope that something would be
said that would help her to establish a connection once again
to her own native religious roots. I asked her if she had found
something in what I had said that was helpful to her. She replied
that indeed she had, that it had to do with my discussion of the
circle as a symbol for totality, and the quotations I had made
from the American Indian Black Elk on the subject of the circle
that held all things together in the power of Wakan Tanka (the
Great Spirit), and that also existed in the human soul. When
she heard this it made a great impression, for this, she said,
was exactly what her own people, the Xhosa, believed about
the circle, and this is why the Xhosa, like the Sioux Indians of
Black Elk's time, made their houses in a circle, and danced in a
circle. "The way it was with the Indians," she said, "is exactly
the way it was with us." Then she knew that the beliefs of her
people were not meaningless superstition but were a symbolic
expression of universal truths, and she felt strengthened. For
although the mind may be satisfied with rational theories, the
soul hungers for images, parables, stories, and myths, which relate us to psychological truth on a deeper level than intellectual
concepts.

For this reason, Hanna Wolff's book not only increases our
knowledge but also strengthens our faith, and nourishes not only
the mind but also the soul. Faith, she explains, does not mean
blind belief, but refers to the capacity of the soul to be open
to life-giving truths. In one of her most brilliant explanations
of a parable she tells of the Sower and the Seed and its inner
meaning. The sower sowed his seed. Some fell on hard ground
and could not take root. Some fell on a path and birds ate it.

Other seed fell on thorny ground and was choked by the thorns. But some seed fell on open and receptive ground, took root, and grew. Readers can read for themselves about the psychological meaning of the hard ground, the birds that eat the seed, and the thorns. The ground that could receive the seed is that quality in a person which the New Testament calls faith; it opens up mind and soul to life-giving psychological truth.

In her "Afterword," Wolff shares with us some of the criticisms that have been leveled at her. One of these is that she is a "prisoner" of the psychology of Carl Jung. That is a strange thing for someone to say. It is true that she is steeped in the psychology of Jung, but she is no prisoner, for a prisoner is confined against his or her will, but she willingly and freely has made Jung's psychology part of her own outlook. The reason she accepted Jung so joyfully is that both Jung and Jesus are talking about the same thing: individuation, that mysterious process that impels and leads a person to become who he or she is meant to be. In religious language, individuation is fulfilling the Will of God. There is no other psychologist in our times who has this idea as Jung has it except for Fritz Kunkel (who, unfortunately, does not appear to be known to Wolff, although both of them are of German origin). Had she viewed Jesus' teaching through the eyes of any other psychology she would not have been able to see its inner meaning. If you look at the world through dark glasses, everything appears dark; if you look at an ancient religious teaching through a myopic psychology you will not be able to see its far-ranging meaning. It also works the other way around: by absorbing the meaning of the teachings of Jesus, we are in certain respects enabled to see more about the nature of the individuation process than even Jung saw.

For this reason Wolff is unabashedly Jungian in her approach. She frequently refers to the numinosity of the processes of the unconscious. She sees dreams as relentlessly portraying for us the truth about the state of our soul in ways that are invaluable for therapy. She sees myth and imagery as treasure houses of wisdom that are able to express nuances of meaning that cannot be contained in a purely rational approach.

On the other hand, while she uses Jung extensively she is

not "schoolistic." She does not try to convert people to Jung —
nor to Jesus for that matter — but only urges them to become
open to their own creative process. Following Jesus' own example she is not interested in whether people officially espouse
either the "correct" psychology or the "correct" religion. It is
who one becomes that matters. Nor is she interested in teaching any particular form of therapy. As she points out, it is not
the technique that matters in therapy, but the therapist. The
therapist himself or herself *is* his or her own method. Everything done in therapy comes from the integrity, consciousness,
and wholeness of the therapist, and in comparison with this the
method is of strictly secondary importance. You might say that
God doesn't know (or care) whether a therapist is a Certified
Jungian or a this-or-that. God is interested in *who* a person is,
not *what* a person is. In this too she follows Jesus himself, who
did not espouse any existing school of thought of his time. The
consciousness of Jesus came directly out of his relationship with
the unconscious; it is not an historically conditioned consciousness, and as a result Jesus taught, healed, and led people as a
unique individual. In the same way, Jesus, as Wolff shows, tries
to lead us to our own uniqueness. And this, of course, makes us
children of God.

Chapter 1

Jesus the Therapist

This book has come out of the experience of psychotherapeutic practice. I had been struck, in the course of my analyses, by the frequency with which I would seize on some biblical expression to designate a psychic phenomenon, or to capsulize an insight that had emerged. Likewise I noticed that former clients whom I chanced to meet would repeatedly say something like, "I can't tell you how much it's meant to me — what you said to me that day." And what had I said that day? Invariably, something Jesus had first said in the pages of the New Testament. There was only one conclusion to be drawn. The speech, activity, and life of Jesus fairly abound with all manner of therapeutic insights. And I began to pursue my impression.

Of course, the objection can be raised: Naturally an analyst who is also a theologian will find a thing or two about analysis in the Bible! And the whole thing becomes a good-natured (or cruel) joke. When objections of that sort arise, I come right out and say: If analysts or their critics ignore their historical and philosophical Christian background, then that is their problem, not mine. Surely there is no such thing as too much associative and scientific background when it comes to understanding intricate psychic phenomena and occurrences.

As my interest grew, so did my grasp of the implications of this discovery. Inescapably, the concept of Jesus as psychotherapist is an appropriate one for the world of our modern conceptions, for our modern state of consciousness — especially in

1

view of the familiarity the notion of psychotherapy enjoys today. And the more closely I examined the New Testament, the
more clearly it emerged: to regard Jesus as a therapist was by
no means a mere faddish, artificial play on popular interests —
a bit of "modern hype," as it were. No, in the pages of the
New Testament we actually find what we refer to today as psychotherapy, and that in the grand manner, utterly valid, and
capable of teaching us modern scientific therapists some things
of crucial importance. But what finally overwhelmed me with
the urgency of pursuing this intuition still further was the insight that Jesus' therapy is practiced against the background
of such a convincing, substantial, and therefore thrilling picture
of the human being. The natural science of today, I could see,
and psychology in particular — with its materialistic positivism,
its interpretation of the human being and the psyche in terms
of a mechanics of collective drive-structures — would do well to
examine this model if it ever hopes to learn what the human
being and the psyche really are (if it is not too late).

To Be a Therapist

As we know, Jesus the therapist actually describes himself as
a physician. Of course, he specifies the character of his clien-
tele. He is a physician not for the healthy, or for those who
think they are healthy, but for the sick who have the courage to
admit that they are sick. There is no quackery here! Here is a
physician who is not speaking out of some sort of vague personal
experience, without any real knowledge of the mighty phenomena in which he dares to interfere. Here is no bungling appeal
to superficial emotivity, that, once it has gotten its clients to
"emote," leaves everything just the way it was. Here is no am-
ateur concentration on symptoms, in the spirit of the methods
that say, "Let's get it done and get out of here." No, Jesus
goes right to the heart of the matter, with determination and
consistency. He delves to the marrow. In no time at all he
sees through mere appearance, mere seeming, and proceeds directly to the inward being of a person. He concerns himself
immediately with what the New Testament calls the "heart" of

a person — the whole human being, body and soul. In no case are his speech and action determined by commonplace academic views, or the "current theory." They are dictated exclusively by empathy, existential engagement, and a preoccupation with total thoroughness. To put it graphically: Jesus is like someone intending to build a house and beginning the work by digging right down to the bedrock. This, in my opinion, is how personality must be established. And this is why Jesus "delved deep" (cf. Mark 2:17, Luke 5:31).[1] What else does the analyst, the therapist, accomplish, or seek to accomplish?[2]

Tradition is unanimous in its impression of Jesus as an extraordinarily well-qualified therapist. "No one had to tell him anything about people. He knew people through and through" (John 2:25). Very simply, he "saw their thoughts" (Matt. 9:4). He likewise "saw" their faith — their trust or their diffidence (Matt. 9:2). He "saw through" their inmost emotions (Mark 12:15). Human beings, in the deepest core of their being, were completely open to him. He would behold them, "see through" them, recognize them for what they were, and at once put his finger on the sore spot: "Fine, very well ... and you know, I like you a lot ... but you have an open wound, and it's a bad one" (cf. Luke 18:22)! Here — for example in the case of the rich young man — we have differential diagnosis from the outset. Obviously Jesus had at his disposition a highly differentiated, all but clairvoyant, intuitive faculty. There was no need for anamnesis and exploration.

People were gripped by Jesus' intuitive powers. They were "grasped" — not sentimentally, but in the way that a penetrating intuition seizes you by the lapels and challenges you, somehow brings you to bay, "tackles" you, brings you up short, in your most personal reality. Your first reaction is a countermovement, psychologically only too understandable, of momentary withdrawal. People were shocked. The crowds, individuals, the disciples, were startled, all of them, over and over again. After this moment of psychological disarming, however, comes the breakthrough — the purifying catharsis that has the potential to bring you to admit that your life is a lie and break with that life. There is something wrong with me, very wrong. I don't even deserve to be in your presence (Luke 5:8). More generally, "We've never seen anything like this" (Mark 2:12), or, "No one ever talked that way before" (John 7:46).

Why not? What is it that makes Jesus' actions and words so unique? Again and again the New Testament gives us the answer. It all comes down to one thing. Jesus spoke and conversed "powerfully," or "with authority." But he never overwhelmed. He never "cut anyone off at the knees," as we say. His words *convinced* (Mark 1:22). And he convinced his addressees not only by his words, but also, and mainly, by the *effect* he had on them. "A healing power came forth from him" (Luke 6:19). *Jesus was himself the therapy that he practiced.*

This is the hallmark of Jesus' *modus procedendi*. And it is a valid basic principle for all psychotherapy. Jesus was his own therapy. We are not Jesus, of course, nor therefore can we hope to be the intermediaries of the precise therapy he applied in the gospel accounts. Obviously we are issuing no invitation to today's therapist to overstep legitimate bounds, to engage in inadmissible generalizations, or to spiritualize scientific analytical therapy. Nothing could be further from our mind in these paragraphs than to reduce, limit, or in any way res trict the personhood and activity of Jesus to that of a therapist. Doubtless I ought to repeat that statement in every chapter, lest I have to hear the pointed reminder that, after all, what Jesus actually wanted to be, and actually was, was "something else again." To be sure. I have no intention of anything but sticking to my last, and if professionals in any other area have "something else again" to say about Jesus, by all means let them say it. However, let them do so "convincingly" — since this is the criterion Jesus expressly demands, and one so easily forgotten in the presence of high-sounding declarations.

But depth psychology is not theology, and it is not metaphysics, and so I set forth what depth psychology can set forth (and I intentionally avoid saying that *only* depth psychology can set it forth). Whether a given text expressly intends to convey the datum of depth psychology that I read out of it, however, is of course neither here nor there. We all constantly express a great deal of material without any notion of its deeper psy-

chic meaning, and yet our statement or reaction *has* this deeper
sense, so that depth psychology is altogether within its rights
to subject our assertion to analytic explicitation and interpretation. As Niederwimmer says, with absolute justice: "If a text
intends something that is open to psychological explicitation,
it is altogether indifferent whether that text intends to have
transmitted it or not."[3] It is a question of objectivity. If a given
meaning is objectively present, then it is open to explicitation.
When it is demonstrably present in the text, even if it is not
stated, the author of the text must take responsibility for it, all
of it, and for the depth psychologist to be satisfied with anything less means doing half a job. We may not rest content with
bungling superficiality. I have no understanding for the faddish
reproach of "psychologization." At any rate none is being practiced here, where we undertake to state only what the text, the
Jesus tradition itself, strictly and recognizably contains, and
can therefore be expressed by depth psychology. It may sound
altogether new, but this is beside the point.

Jesus was his own therapy, as we have observed. This principle is (or ought to be) a general one, valid for any therapist.
And so we already have a first basis for agreement with Jesus
the therapist. To put it another way: therapists can help their
clients only to the extent that they themselves, the therapists,
have achieved integration — self-becoming, or individuation. *No
analysis outstrips its analyst.* The "measure of the clarification
of meaning" of which we are capable is conditioned by the extent to which we are transparent to ourselves.[4] Carl Jung, in
particular, has called attention to this important truth. Time
and time again, although without drawing it directly from the
New Testament, Jung fairly hammers it in: the therapist is his
or her own method and therapy. This is a basic principle, and
the foundation of Jung's demand that every analyst undergo
analysis, a demand he was the first to make.

This principle is explicit in Jesus' own therapeutic approach.
We see it in that all but clairvoyant intuition of his, which simply gripped his contemporaries. Now it has been recognized as
a therapeutic imperative of our own time, as we are endeavoring
to make clear in these paragraphs. It has put us to the question

with an insistence that brooks no evasion. Jesus sees us through
and through, pierces us to the quick, and demands: Who are
you, you the analyst, that you assume as an objective right,
arrogate to yourselves as your purpose, and feel yourselves intimately justified in doing so, the plumbing of the depths of this
patient's soul? What is the state of your own, personal "self-
transparency"? Authentic therapist that he is, Jesus reminds
us that all analysis begins with a self-critique, continues in the
company of self-analysis, and ends with the same. The process
is never broken off. Do we wish to see that? Do we, with all
of our intellectualisms, our drive-mechanisms, and our often so
petty intent to "bring out in the open" and "unmask" the inner
phenomena of our patients' souls — do we wish to see that?

Clarification of a Basic Principle

When I call Jesus a psychotherapist I mean exactly what I say.
There is nothing cheap or modish in my intent here or modish
in my design, I repeat, no sham appeal to the fashion of the
times, no pretense to an intricate, brilliant insight that really
only betrays a purely superficial "modernity." No, when I call
Jesus a psychotherapist I mean "psychotherapist" in the precise, objective meaning that the designation "psychotherapist"
actually has *today*. Jesus underwent no analysis. He tells us
nothing of neurosis, trauma, or depression. Our modern conceptual inventory is obviously absent from the pages of the New
Testament. What really counts, however, is a knowledge of the
live-enhancing and life-destroying psychic processes, and this Jesus has in abundance. This is so authentically, so solidly present
in his words and actions that we, today's therapists, can still
learn from it. After all, depth psychology, which creates a crucial turning point in any discourse on the human being, actually
drawing a line of demarcation between eras of human existence,
has had no choice but to develop on the cultural basis determined by the impulse of Jesus. That the individual researcher
not happen to know this, indeed not even bother to gainsay it
(never having heard of it), is of no consequence. The positivistic, materialistic, and Marxist pomposities that cut so wide a

swath today, even in depth psychology, really only represent a
wholesale psychic regression and consequent narrowing of our
horizon of comprehension. There never was the least possibility
that this sort of "science" could so much as begin to deal with
theses such as we have just enunciated.

Accordingly, we practice *no conceptual counterfeiting* when
we speak of Jesus as a psychotherapist. I am well aware, then,
that I place myself altogether at odds with all of those manifold
efforts of our time that would like to befriend depth psychology
in a "nice and easy," superficial, comfortable way. Is there any
end to the list of self-styled "therapy" groups and circles that
cannot hold a candle to depth psychology, for all their inflation
at the hands of the media? "Do it yourself" is their watchword,
and their name is legion.

Even the church and theology connive. We have no choice
but to mention this, in view of the nature of the problem with
which we are concerned. Long after this book was conceived I
participated in a Catholic "workshop," billed as a seminar on
"Jesus as Therapist." There a historian of religion, who was
also a dogmatic theologian, expounded on the New Testament
account of the calming of the storm. Without so much as a nod
in the direction of the basic elements of literary criticism, this
gentleman presented what he thought to be the basic meaning
of the pericope: in quieting the storm, "Jesus the Therapist"
heals the rift that sunders the world. And on and on he went
in the spirit of the old, indeed the oldest, Catholic allegorical
exegesis. Then paintings were displayed, representing Jesus in
various ways as a "wonder-worker." They all illustrated con-
ceptualizations that preoccupied the early church Fathers, and
surely enough, for each painting, we heard a passage from Saint
Augustine by way of interpretation. Last of all a single painting from the baroque period was presented, portraying Jesus
realistically as an actual physician in some actual person's sick-
room. Not a word was said about realism. Instead, the painting
was criticized as representative of the "emergence of Manner-
ism." In brief, what was offered here was the oldest of dusty
dogmatism — under the shameless title "Jesus as Therapist"!

Nor is the situation in the Protestant church a great deal

different. Here the function of depth psychology is "to help
in a psychological concretion of the kerygma."[5] It provides a
new "hermeneutic key."[6] It is most welcome, then, and has the
potential to bolster biblical or dogmatic propositions. It can
be utilized to concretize or reinforce our persuasion that the
kerygma affords real, existential encounter. Look, it says, the
kerygma is right on target! For example, depth psychology can
now be used as an aid to homiletics. There is some truth here.
We must think through, from scratch, *the objective content* of
what we say, in light of the new awareness afforded by depth
psychology today. But here again, in actual practice depth psychology is kept at arm's length. The easier way is: you exploit
it, you sack it, you toss around a few technical terms, you "do"
depth psychology. You brandish it a bit — just enough to falsify
objectivity and guarantee your sham modernity.

I have a counter-proposal. Instead of falling victim to this
basically irresponsible, sham modernity, let us be honest with
ourselves. Let us do justice to the change in our awareness that
separates us from the New Testament mind-set. Not even the
new wine of psychoanalytic theory can be pressured into old bot-
tles, however surreptitiously and underhandedly. If, then, the
following pages hold but little in the way of an application of old
formulae and familiar expressions, let readers not at once wrin-
kle their dogmatic brow, but rather let them ask whether the
state of the question, and the state of the facts, under consideration here cannot perhaps be better translated into categories
of our modern awareness. If they can, we shall have only gained
a boon.

I have attempted just such a transposition of the New Testament data concerning the figure of Jesus to the level of our
modern consciousness in my *Jesus der Mann: Die Gestalt Jesu
in tiefenpsychologischer Sicht.*[7] The present volume is intended
as the complement to that work. As my earlier piece demonstrated that Jesus was a modern man — an "integrated" man,
in psychological terms — now we pose the question: How does
such a man behave? How does he deal with his neighbor? *How
did Jesus manage to have such a dynamic, healing hold on people,* so that it was reported that "power flowed from him, and

he healed them all" (Luke 5:17)? We are in the presence of the impression that enabled a Rembrandt, in his "Hundred Guilder Print," to portray such a gripping sense of "today." Let us investigate what made this impression possible.[8]

Chapter 2

The Will to Be Well

"How is it that this strange talk never grows tiresome?" asks
Ernst Bloch. And he answers his own question: Biblical discourse is truly remarkable in this sense. Somehow it takes aim
and strikes what matters. It is "speech as address, as appeal."[1]
Thus one is "taken" with it at once, seized existentially, with
the inevitability of bedrock. And what is true of biblical utterance in general holds for the discourse of Jesus in particular.
But with these observations we are still very far from an adequate characterization of what is so special about Jesus' speech.
We grasp the special quality of Jesus' manner of address only
through an examination of the special manner of his therapeutic
speech and behavior. The first, the elementary question Jesus
asks is invariably: "Do you really want to be well?"

Do You Want to Be Well?

Do you really want to be well? Jesus initiates his dialogue with
the cripple of Bethesda with this question (John 5:1–17). For
thirty-eight years this individual has languished by the side of
the intermittent therapeutic bath. But he has never been able
to bathe. Infallibly, the crowd jostles him aside and he is left
out! At least this is what he says. The circumstances are heart-
rending, and Jesus' question, "Do you want to be well," seems
shockingly out of place. It is at least arresting, and may seem
downright tactless. But Jesus' reading of his patient's account

is apparently anything but identical with the intent of that account. Jesus' inquiry into the state of the paralytic's affect is well advised. "Do you *want* to be well?" he asks. This is the *primary, cardinal question* in any therapy.

Our Johannine account is in keeping with the whole tenor of the New Testament in this respect. To the Canaanite woman, for example, who has approached Jesus in behalf of her suffering daughter, Jesus responds, after some initial feather-rustling: "Your trust is truly great. Let it happen to you as you will" (Matt. 15:28). The woman's persistence brooks no rejection. In all trust, she simply insists. And this shows Jesus that she really "wills." Or we may consider Jesus' parable of the widow who is refused the justice of the courts. Instead of desisting from her appeal, her struggle, she "just doesn't let go," as a modern German translation would have it, until the judge finally grants her what is hers by right (Luke 18:1–8). People should not let go, Jesus is teaching us. They should really *will* — they should will and will again. Otherwise it would be better simply to drop the matter. Jesus finds the rich young man a likeable sort, but the youth suddenly pulls back when Jesus touches him where it hurts — in his pocketbook. Jesus looks back in sorrow on Jerusalem. He has done so much, he has cared so much. But "you didn't want it" (Matt. 23:37).

This is the fine spirit that becomes typical of Christianity in the age of voluntarism, a main current of Christian development culminating in Augustine and Luther. Rudolf Bultmann sums it up: In the mind of early Christianity, the essence of the human being does not lie in logos and reason, as Hellenism had thought, but rather:

> If one addresses to ancient Christianity the question where it *does* lie, then, the answer can only be: in the will. At all events, being-human — life as human life — is always understood as an eagerness, a striving, a determination and willingness.[2]

In other words: "A ready acceptance in words has no value; an act of will is required."[3]

Just so with analysis. And yet how easily this is overlooked.

Medical or clinical therapy is regarded as a service *to* clients. We surround our clients with all manner of "care." We cast them in a passive role from start to finish. They do not *want* to *get* well; they want to be *made* well. The enormous currency of mind-altering drugs has rendered this mind-set all but universal. The notion that an untoward psychic development that may have been years in the making cannot be quickly and successfully corrected by taking a few pills is an attitude as novel for most patients as it is uncomfortable.

Third-Party Referrals

What the client first of all, and all too often, really "wants" in analysis can be sketched under a few typical categories. Let us begin with third-party referrals. A husband will telephone: "It's about my wife — she really needs help!" Wives find their husbands to be in the same need, of course. Or parents will report: "We've really done our best. There's nothing more we can do. Our son (or daughter) needs your help." A man will want to separate from his lover, usually because she is "frigid." Or *she* will think she must send *him* off for "therapy," very often on account of his allegedly boundless sexual appetite, and even more often because of his "impotence." But it is simply impossible for one party to escort, haul, or pressure another into analytical therapy. I learned very quickly that third-party referrals are invariably unavailing. In fact, only too often it is the person making the referral that really needs help. Here we see the crucial importance of the "you." Do *you* want to be well? Is this *your* desire? That reach for the phone, that autonomous declaration of your *own* need — this is the first step. This act of courage and initiative, this *will*, constitutes the indispensable prerequisite for a hopeful therapeutic outcome. Basic spontane-ity — a minimal personal commitment — is the necessary condi-tion for an auspicious start. Either you make the first contact of your own free will, and with a minimum of commitment, or the therapy will not even get off the ground. Spontaneity is absolutely necessary in terms of an *initial commitment*.

A boarding school student had made a suicide attempt.[4] Her headmistress, her school, her mother, had all risen to the occasion, with a sense of urgency, with love, and with perseverance. Money was no object. At first the girl seemed to go along. But eventually she began to find excuses to postpone or cancel her sessions. This occurred more and more frequently, until finally one day she came right out and said: "I'm fine. I don't want this at all. My mother wants it." (But that was no help to *her*.)

A marriage was in difficulties. The wife thought the husband simply could not go on without therapy. And indeed he began to come for therapy. Then he had a dream. A single dream — to be sure, a very basic one — in the course of our discussion, ushered in a sudden blockage. That is, the man's dream activity ceased, quite abruptly, in the face of massive resistance. A more intensive exploration provoked a spontaneous outburst: "I don't want any more therapy! It's my wife who wants me to come to therapy!" At the basis of the marriage problem was the husband's massive attachment to his mother. In his dream, the furnace in his house would not work properly. As soon as it would start up it would immediately shut down. The dream continued: the man left the house to get into his car and go for help — and to his dismay saw that his mother had gone off with his car! Warmth represents feeling. The patient's capacity for feeling was underdeveloped: no sooner did it "start up" than it cooled. The man's attachment to his mother proved to be overwhelming. He requested that his analysis be terminated, and there was nothing to do but to accede. The question is whether *you* want to be well.

Misused Analysis

The most frequent problems are presented by a misused analysis. This time the emphasis is on the word "well." No, the client's ambitions do not go that far. They consist of one or more altogether specific goals. But the heart of analytical therapy is the furtherance of personality formation, via the removal of blockages or the correction of unhealthy developments that may have come into the picture, in order to get the patient's psyche once more into creative flux. Then the particular symptoms constituting the occasion of the original complaint are found to correct themselves entirely. They disappear "of themselves," or "incidentally." Now, by no means does the candidate whose heart is set on an extraneous goal want all of that! Instead the intent will be very narrowly specified. Analyses bound to extraneous goals constitute a misapplication, an abuse, of the analytic process. They pursue aims that lie outside the patient — aims, then, that an analysis correctly under way would probably actually fail to endorse. The attitudes of the unconscious would veto the goal and shut down the analytic process. Goal-bound analysis is taking the dowry and sending the bride packing.

The most drastic case I ever had was that of a man who had been sentenced to prison. He came to my office, accompanied by his tearful wife, to beg me to receive him into therapy. I did so, although it cost me a great deal of time in negotiations and consultations with the district courts and the state attorney's office. To all appearances, I was dealing with an extremely willing analysand. But then he managed to obtain an interview at the Ministry, and in view of special circumstances, including my intercession in his behalf, the prospect of a commutation arose. My client's prison sentence might become a fine. At once his interest in any analytical treatment vanished. The therapy had achieved its goal — or better, *his* goal — and was abruptly terminated.

The naiveté with which people sometimes begin analysis, for the most outlandish purposes, can be downright tragicomic. A certain white-collar worker, with the utmost assurance, expected analysis to furnish him with additional personal qualities that would enable him to get the best of his competitors for an upcoming promotion.

We may usually expect analysis undertaken in a judicial context, especially in connection with divorce proceedings, to fall under the category of analysis misapplied for extraneous purposes. A divorced man came to me for therapy. He was perfectly correct, from his opening greeting to his polite leave-taking. He understood it all. He was willingness personified. What do you do with an analysand who understands everything but is obviously letting none of it "get to him"? One day I surprised him

with the question, "But why are you going to all this trouble?"
"Why, to have custody of the children!" came the prompt answer. I'm doing *so* much! I can't be such a bad fellow, now,
can I? Analysis was supposed to further this impression with
the court.

Milieu-Direction

Milieu-direction is another, and anything but rare, circumstance
that will undermine the success of an analysis. Sooner or later,
authentic analytical therapy will come to the threshold of genuine self-development, real self-becoming, a truthful grasp of
oneself. Now the client's behavior will change. This will become
evident to all concerned. And then oh! — the disapproval, the
frenzy, and the anger! Dare to change, and, depend on it, there
will be a fuss. Suddenly the image I have of my son, my husband,
my employee, my neighbor, and so on, is no longer a true picture
of that person. This arouses displeasure, to say the least. Let
a woman genuinely develop her personality, says Jung, and the
other women of the neighborhood will all be sure to run up to
her shrieking and raving and begging her to stop this nonsense!
The deeper cause of their consternation, of course, is their per-
turbation at having their own personhoods called in question.
If only analysis could work a mere "adaptation"! Let it make
it easier for a person to function in his or her de facto environment! But "adaptation" (the question is always, "Adaptation to
what?") can be the ruin of a personality for good and all. And
so one's "next of kin become one's enemies" (Matt. 10:36) — "a
person's enemies suddenly live in the same house," as Luther
translates. We are truly astonished at the precision of Jesus'
depth of insight when we see his addressees' reactions in terms
of genuine depth psychology. Painful confrontation with a stubborn environment is unavoidable, no matter how prudently or
tactfully patients emerging from therapy may demonstrate their
new-found ability to take responsibility for themselves. And
these newly healed persons by no means always hold their own
against the resistance of their surroundings.

   We may occasionally like to think it expedient to involve a

father, a mother, a spouse, or the like, in a client's therapeutic process. This temptation will most often occur when the persons concerned are plainly the cause of our client's psychic ills. As a rule, we shall be well advised to keep the family at the greatest possible distance from the treatment. Freud's situation is amusing. "Ask yourself now how many surgical operations would turn out successfully if they had to take place in the presence of all the members of the patient's family, who would stick their noses into the field of the operation and exclaim aloud at every incision. In psychoanalytic treatments the intervention of relatives is a positive danger...."[5] More soberly, Freud cites the fact that relatives, through their spontaneous verbal interference, can actually stifle an analysis altogether. The analyst must be consistent and energetic here. The "assistant" that really makes the difference is the unconscious. Under certain circumstances, it will utter loud protests precisely against outside interference.

When analysts falter in their undeviating attention to the declarations of the analysand's unconscious, there is no little danger of a falsification of their own procedure. Interference on the part of their client's milieu touches mainly, or at least in equal measure, the analyst, who will now become the target of a veritable fusillade of raillery. "Go back to your surrogate mother," a spiteful wife will sneer at a patient. "My husband is furious with you," an analysand will report, timidly, and she will begin to lose interest in her therapy. "I'm beginning to wonder who needs therapy, you or your analyst!" thunders a wrathful husband. The analyst has acquired the knack of coping with milieu pressure professionally and with a certain amount of humor. It is not so easy for the analysand!

A clerical worker had made brilliant strides with his therapy. To boot, the creative powers of his unconscious were so stirred that, in quick succession, he wrote a pair of highly acclaimed literary pieces. "I could never have thought of all those things without the therapy," he averred. The outward result was an important promotion. In his marriage, too, and in his relationship with his children, all was going very well. The only person to be dissatisfied was his elderly mother-in-law, until now the autocrat of the extended family and unable to resign herself to a change of such proportions in the network of households. And so she came to my office. The floodgates of her anguish burst. Then she opened her purse, produced a thousand-mark bill, and declared: "Here, please make our Alfred the way he was." Unfortunately, I had to let all that money slip through my fingers.

In a particularly tragic, potentially lethal case, a young girl came to me in great difficulties. It would be improper to delineate the details, but her chronic, lifelong psychosomatic illness had obvious connections with her problem parents, especially her father, who occupied quite a high governmental position. The parents were most status-conscious, and in their minds the father ought to have been at least President of the State by now, although that goal was still a long way off. Eventually I explained the utmost urgency of a consultation with the father. The mother bristled at the very suggestion. "My husband would *never* do a thing like that! What if he were to be seen?" In vain I reminded her that some parents sacrificed, for example, a kidney for their child and barely gave it a second thought. Up to this point the girl had gladly come to therapy and was making remarkable progress. But from this time on she was never allowed to come again. All contact was broken off. This analysis was not just milieu-directed, but milieu-annihilated.

Here we are faced with an age-old, universal psychic reaction. In an ideologically or religiously transmogrified collectivity, or a politically sterile, anesthetized society, suddenly the pure voice of truth sounds forth. In former times the reaction was stoning or crucifixion. Today it is character assassination. The fact that the reaction is a primitive, collective one, of immemorial antiquity, is scarcely a consolation when you have to watch an innocent young person being heartlessly sacrificed to the petty spirit of her elders' milieu.

Intellectualized Analysis

Another attempt to evade the authentic therapeutic process is constituted by intellectualized analysis. This is an approach that infiltrates, in particular, so-called academic analysis. The natural scientist or the physician thinks, "I'll just [!] go through an academic analysis. It'll help me professionally, later on. I'll just study analysis the way I learned anatomy or tissue disease." The basic scientific attitude in the latter areas of medicine is and must be one of "distantiation," of course — a strictly objective, neutral approach. But now our scientist is suddenly expected to demonstrate fantasy and intuition, have ideas of an irrational character, enter upon an altogether personal engagement, think and even behave in an existentially committed fashion.

Suddenly the "academic" analysand begins to notice that, after all, analysis is analysis and bears on the patient! Our "researcher" comes to the abrupt realization that this so-called academic analysis is basically no different from an analysis that may be medically necessary — say, to help someone who is suffering with a neurosis. This insight is downright humiliating, and has been the reef of many a shipwreck. A goodly number of these analysands, however, take their new troubles valiantly in hand, and eventually avow that the whole study of medicine has acquired a new, creative value for them.

These same enthusiasts for academic analysis would also like us to pressure the large percentage of young people who manifest a certain instability, the ones who would not dare to make a commitment for anything in the world, to prove that they are a "real man" or a "real woman" by undertaking analysis. Youth, however, are as garrulous as the day is long. They know nothing, and so much the better. They are perfectly sure that this or that approach will never do — that it is simply impossible, just on theoretical grounds. And indeed "theoretical" is the basic vocable of their flimsy intellectualism. What they would like is for analysis to verify their theories. Their vacuity where meaning is concerned, the debility of their existence, is incapable of reaching for more than this, at least for the moment. Unless the analyst maintains a critical spirit, and holds the line, this new type of analysand can drown an analysis in the twinkling of an eye.

And yet I would not simply turn away, or browbeat, any of these weaklings. They are frustrated to the marrow of their bones. Even these cases can turn into particularly successful, gratifying experiences.

A young doctor in residency had learned everything psychotherapy had to offer. And he was a real chatterbox — that bane of the therapist. I found the analysis a great strain, and by the end of a session my nerves were decidedly on edge. He hardly ever had a dream to report. But shortly before the end of the number of sessions he had requested, something happened. It was as if someone had grasped the steering wheel of a moving vehicle and spun it completely around. In his own words: "Believe me, I'm finished thinking analysis will do for me what I have to do for myself." And surely enough, after all of those wasted semesters he not only got down to business for the first time, but earned a hefty commendation. At long last — he had learned to work!

Analysis with Reservations

Analysis with reservations is a good name for the type of enterprise frequently undertaken by another group of persons who, like the clients we have already seen, are not really ready to answer Jesus' opening query in the affirmative. They want to evade the question. They recoil from the answer. These analysands would like to open up indeed, but only within predetermined bounds. Of course, without realizing it, these patients have written their own lunch check, without benefit of consultation with the innkeeper. The innkeeper, in the present instance, is the unconscious, which brings to light, rejects or recommends, urges or declines, only and precisely what it pleases, without the least bother about what we ourselves would like to hear. It proclaims whatever *it* holds to be needful for the maintenance or reestablishment of psychic balance — the things that our everyday consciousness is often precisely most in the dark about. Otherwise we should never get to such and such particular neuroses, compulsions, depressions, and so forth.

I am very well aware that many analysts do not know or acknowledge the unconscious in its autonomous compensatory functionality. To these therapists we can only say: When dis-

coveries are made, they are made. If you refuse to accept them,
then we can only abide by Hegel's recommendation and go on
without you.

What we have styled "analysis with reservations" is equally
benighted with respect to any connections of this sort. Here
too the concern is to keep the reins out of the hands of the
unconscious. One has no idea that the unconscious will infallibly
snatch them away.

A schoolteacher's sexual problems had made her so uncom-
monly prudish that her analysis had completely stalled. Whenever an awkward point would arise she would give her stereo-
typed response: "I shouldn't care to discuss that just now."
But fortunately she had a powerful dream, quite early in her
treatment, and her dream showed her her general attitude with
compelling transparency. She dreamed that someone said to
her: "You rattle your chains, but you don't want to talk." In
view of her dream, this analysand admitted that no, she had
never imagined anything of the kind. But all she did about
it was to keep rattling her chains. That is, she broke off the
analysis. Her dream was the drastic symbol of the condition of
untold thousands of persons who suffer but who *do not want to
be helped.*

Enthusiasts for meditation groups, members of transcenden-
tal experience circles or other superficial methods for "getting
in contact with yourself," tend as a rule to seek analysis with
reservations — which is no analysis at all.

But no rigid rules can be laid down. I once had two nuns
in analysis. The analyses were successful. They had been undergone without any reservations. But one of the consequences
was that both sisters, entirely independently of each other, left
their order. It was scarcely my fault. It was the unconscious
that had made this demand on them.

The instance of the two nuns brings to mind a further varia-
tion of "analysis with reservations" that is important not only in
itself, but for our general topic. I refer to a particular hesitation
encountered among theologians and practicing Christians. This
reservation runs rather as follows. "Analysis? No, thank you.
Analysis will destroy your faith. Analysis tears down rather

than building. That's its natural tendency." What are we to say of this reservation, in terms of which a potential analysand often manifests such decided distantiation?

A first, honest response to objections of this kind is that yes, of course there are therapists of a nihilistic, materialistic, or positivistic persuasion, and in their hands analysis becomes a lethal weapon. In the understanding — or lack thereof — of such analysts, analysis is to all intents and purposes capsulized in slogans like: "Out of the cloister! Out of the church!" But such analysts do not really analyze at all. They squeeze and compress their analysands' psyches into their own paltry schemata, which their human immaturity and half-baked science have the gall to set forth and represent as absolute.

I use the term "immaturity" advisedly. Every debate with positivistic analysts like those under consideration has shown me that they understand nothing whatever of matters of faith, and have no notion of the figure of Jesus (especially where the broad, newer international research is concerned), which, after all, is what is basically at stake. They have assimilated only a few intellectualisms concerning what they call religion, and this is the dead horse they so tirelessly beat. Such analysts are a genuine danger, yes. One can only run from them, for they are capable of engineering immeasurable psychic harm, as I have seen only too well in the course of my own practice.

Every personality is like a well-cut precious stone. It has many facets. It is the unhappy circumstance of Freud himself to have exhibited, along with other sides of his personality, the dark side as well, the side whose facets gleam with only the seeming light of a mirage. The Freudian writing most often cited in the present context is his *The Future of an Illusion*.[6] Here Freud simply denies that religion has a future at all. That is scarcely of any concern to a Christian, however, since Jesus taught no "religion" in the Freudian sense, so that Freud's somber prognoses simply do not touch him. Mitscherlich holds that this work of Freud is to be ranged not so much under the category of psychology as under that of the history of religions, and that therefore it is under this aspect that it ought to be judged. However, Mitscherlich overlooks the fact that precisely no specialist in religion would ever even give Freud's lucubrations serious consideration, as indeed none ever has. The scholarship that has formed an abstract concept of "religion," adopting the conceptualization so dear to the Enlightenment and popularized by the same, has embraced a notion to which nothing corresponds in the concrete, historical order.[7]

There are, to be sure, various *attitudes of faith,* named for their founder, their core notion, or the like — Buddhism, Jainism, Arya Dharma, Hinduism, Islam — literally "Surrender" — and so on. But there is simply no such thing as "religion" in the concrete, historical order, and certainly none of the manifold attitudes of faith is willing to be called, precisely in modern times, anything like "religion" in this abstract sense. Authentic attitudes of faith are happy to leave this empty, useless notion to Western intellectualism, and it is not difficult to see why. This is a broad subject, and we can consider it here only in the form of the present series of thesis-like propositions. But the latter suffice for our purposes, which is to explain our designation of materialism or positivism in analytical psychology as ignorance and infantilism, and our rejection of them as unscientific attitudes.[8]

Naturally, to the extent that a person's "religion" were to consist of an artificial, desperate, spasmodic clinging to empty intellectual propositions of this sort, that person's religion would not be a faith attitude at all for it would not be rooted in life. And yes, it would be sure to collapse in analysis. But this is a good thing, since an abstract religion deserves no more. When we speak of "analysis with reservations" as a misuse of analysis, then, let us not fixate on the client alone. Let us turn our regard to the analyst, as well, and the possible negative, destructive reservations that he or she only too often entertains in matters pertaining to an attitude of faith.

Analysand and analyst alike have one job to do, and one only: to enter upon a positively critical confrontation with the psychic information mounting up out of the unconscious of them both. In other words the pair have the task of pursuing the self-expression of the psyche, which, especially in problem situations, will go its own, autonomous way.

Where a person's life is constructed and supported by a deep, inner attitude of faith, an analysis can result only in unsurmised enrichment, broadening, and consolidation. Genuine values are never destroyed.

In a series of brief characterizations, we have spoken of analyses emerging from third-party referrals, analyses misused for extraneous ends, analyses directed by the cultural milieu, analyses that are intellectualized, and finally, analyses undertaken with reservations. These are the principal guises under which a person fails really to respond with a genuine "yes" to Jesus' inquiry whether he or she wishes to "get well."

Then let us return to the paralytic of Bethesda, whom Jesus has now healed (John 5:1–17). Does he belong to one of these "problem groups" — or perhaps to some other, since our list could easily have been longer? Most assuredly. The sufferer's response to Jesus' opening question is strikingly rich in information of interest for depth psychology. Asked whether he really "wants to be well," how does he respond? Instead of answering, in some way, "Surely I do! Yes, of course!" he commences a tale of woe — essentially, a complaint against "others." I can't! "They" won't let me! And this, to be sure, is an altogether typical response, so that we are completely justified in regarding a great many of Jesus' parables and actions as *paradigms in depth psychology.* Patients always begin by talking about "the others." Only with difficulty are they brought to speak of themselves. However, this self-justifying, self-endorsing finger of guilt, pointing to the misunderstanding husband, the wife "you can't talk to," the "hard-to-describe" mother-in-law, and so on, is then, happily, and often very quickly, cut off through dreams that abruptly alter the therapeutic situation. Dreams, after all, speak not of others, but of the dreamer. And they do so in a way that is always surprising, as well as, often enough, a perfect bull's-eye where the patient's particular problem is concerned.

After all, the answer given by our man from Bethesda is totally unbelievable. Really now, are we to believe that in thirty-eight years there was no one to be found, no helpful person, no supporting crutch, to assist this sufferer down to the baths? I have already remarked that the quality of surprise — given the context — attached to Jesus' question is surely intentional on his part. One must know the East in order to understand the behavior of beggars and handicapped persons. Beneath many a ragtag exterior, attracting such a rich flow of alms, is someone with a very nice bank account. Once one has become accustomed to living from alms, one's quality of life is far from the worst, and a beggar or handicapped person is often duly utilized as the principal breadwinner of the extended family. At the same time one's standard of living is guaranteed by the mendicant guilds or castes. But now our mendicant is suddenly well! He must go to work! He must shoulder responsibility. He must altogether change his attitude. Is he so exceedingly happy about that? It would appear not. At any rate he manifests no gratitude whatever. On the contrary, when Jesus' enemies wish to make use of this cure for their own purposes, in order to pin something on Jesus, the paralytic instantly turns against his benefactor and becomes a delator. Jesus chances to meet him again, and gives him a warning. He may have gotten out of this one. But he had better be careful. Something still more evil, more gross, could yet befall him (see John 5:14).

The outcome of this particular treatment is eminently instructive, and for a particular reason. We are actually dealing with a failed therapy here — hence Jesus' earnest animadversion, a unique one from this point of view. The despicable comportment of the sometime cripple, immediately subsequent to his restoration to physical health, leaves little to be desired as a clear demonstration that he is anything but restored to health in the more profound sense of having changed as a person. What we have here is what we would today call a failed "treatment" of symptoms. But this is the way people are, and this is the sober realism that pervades Jesus' therapy. In other words, Jesus is an extraordinary therapist indeed, but he is not a magician. No authentic therapist is, and our pericope shows this very well.

Since this is the "way people are" — since they need a good, hard shove if their treatment is to get anywhere — Jesus is unflagging, energetic, and determined in his appeal to their willingness to change. Our mild, soft, even mawkish image of Jesus is entirely the work of our own projection, in the form of wishful thinking. Cowardly or primitive self-endorsement would of course be happy with a Jesus in that image. But by no means does Jesus fit that image. The very first word of Jesus handed down to us is an unheard-of demand, or appeal: "Change!" (Matt. 4:17). And this mighty call pervades the New Testament tradition from beginning to end. "Go to the trouble,..." he says, disturbing any lethargy (Matt. 7:13). "Ask," "seek," "knock" (Matt. 7:7). But under no conditions think that too much is being asked of you. Now, stop "looking so glum!" (Matt. 6:16). "Get busy" and "turn away" from what you used to be (Matt. 18:3). "Be ever ready" to change, through and through (Luke 12:40). The challenge issued by Jesus — "Do you want to be well?" — is a call for change. Our patient has not understood that. Jesus comes to us with an elementary, difficult demand. That demand has been dogmatized into thin air, to make way for a view of grace as be-all and end-all. No, Jesus addresses a startling appeal to the will to make a total change in the subject.

"You'd like to bask a while in his light," the Gospel of John recalls (John 5:35). You want a sympathetic, reassuring treatment of your symptoms. Sorry, we don't carry that here. Here we launch the human being. The decisive element, then, is the will that grips the whole being, with the intent to restore the human person to the status of sovereign in his or her own psychic household. Our Christian discourse forgets the basic characteristic of Jesus' approach much too much. We had rather preach solidarity, communion in one humanity, comfort and consolation, aid and assistance, fidelity, bearing one another's burdens, and so on. But Jesus' appeal is to a human being's will to change. The question, "Do you want to be well?" calls for a forthright "Yes!" by way of a response. The case is precisely the same with analysis. Analysis, too, ultimately seeks to lead human beings to the truth about themselves, and thus to change and conversion. It too demands a will to change. This is why we have designated the commitment of the free will the absolutely indispensable initial commitment for any analysis.

Resistance

"Do you want to be well?" This single question, understood in the depth of its reference as used by Jesus, may be regarded as a summary and compendium of all that Jesus said and did. At all events it is a question calculated to stir a rebellion. Uncompromisingly it calls for an inner, and then an outer, restructuring, a becoming-new that can only be compared to a psychic revolution. At the very least there is a production quota to be filled, a struggle to be waged.

Where so much is demanded, resistance arises, as surely is to be expected. It may be gentle resistance, or it may be strident. Not seldom it will be coarse, furious, and fanatic. The deeper the psychic level being addressed, or, on the other side, the higher the integration value in view, the more wildly and uninhibitedly will the resistance flail its metaphorical arms.

Let us examine this resistance more closely. In depth psychology we distinguish between *conscious* and *unconscious* resistance, and then again between the *individual* resistance of a single person and the *collective* resistance of a mass of persons. Jesus had to deal with each of these kinds of resistance. It was the collective resistance of the masses, however, especially as he encountered it in the religious hierarchy of his people in those times, that brought him down to death.

Where *conscious resistance* is concerned, Jesus knows he must meet it perceptively, forthrightly, to the point, trenchantly, and adroitly. As a matter of fact, Jesus' adroitness at repartee is astonishing. No ifs, ands, or buts. He comes right to the point, whether he is confronted with a sincere desire, or a hypocritical trick question intended to bring him down with its craft and deceit. Examples abound. The entire New Testament is an example. Let us cite only the coin of tribute (Matt. 22:15–22). "Is it right to pay taxes to the Roman Emperor?" Now, there is a trick question for you. If he says yes, he will have every patriot in the country against him. If he says no, he can be denounced to the Roman authorities forthwith. Yet he makes no attempt to avoid the question. In fact his answer is unambiguous and trenchant. Let's see the coin. Take a look at the image stamped on it. So. The coin is Caesar's. Then give Caesar what you owe him. No question about it. There *is* a question, though, about the image stamped on *you*. What about that? What about the image of God that you are? Do you pay *God* the "duty" you owe God? Do you pay it as you should? I've really wanted to talk to you about that!

And instantly it is the questioners who are in question, and on the deepest level. It is the inquisitors who must come up with an answer. They owe a response. They are in default. "They were dumbfounded, and harassed him no further." But Jesus "harassed" *them* further! Even in conscious resistance, resistance that manifests itself openly, Jesus discovers the hidden motive. To him that motive is only too transparent, and he brings it straight out in the open. "Why this false front? You're just trying to trap me!"

But it is not only in his adversaries that Jesus encounters resistance. In his friends, however, his followers, his sympathizers, the resistance is deep, and hidden. It is *unconscious*. The most opaque figure in this respect has always been that of Judas. Not even contemporary scholarship has been able to sort him out. Why? Because "unconscious" really means unconscious. The subject is actually unaware of a deep, inner resistance. And the more unconscious the resistance, the more it will dig in its heels, so to speak, the more casually it will be able to frustrate our actions, numb the object of our willing, blur the goal of our striving to the point of invisibility. Now we no longer even see our purpose. Unless we can *discover* this sick, neurotic resistance, neither, obviously, shall we be able to deal with it. We modern therapists discover it thanks to the complex apparatus of depth psychology. Jesus discovered it through a personal intuitive faculty of his own. Let us look at a few examples of this faculty at work.

An unconscious resistance is evidently at hand in the cripple of Bethesda — whose story thus continues as our therapeutic paradigm in this chapter. The events ensuing upon his cure demonstrate this. He denounces Jesus to his enemies (John 5:11). A nasty trick, and unthinkable except for the presence of unconscious resistance in the subject.

Again, we find neurotic resistance in the incident of the ten lepers (Luke 17:11–19). Only one returns. He thanks Jesus effusively. But Jesus remarks, "I cleansed ten. Where are the other nine?" Something kept the others from coming back. What it was in their conscious minds we do not know. But it was evidently accompanied by a resistance so strong that they were unable to do what the tenth leper did automatically.

A neurotic resistance is demonstrated by the wealthy youth who asks what he must do to be saved (Mark 10:17-31). Jesus responded so harshly that the youth "was disconcerted, and went away sad." Of course, he had no notion of the real reason for his decision to turn around and walk away. The real reason, after all, was not that he had "many possessions," but that, as Luther says, they had become his idol. He fails to suspect that it is he who has thrown up a hopeless block. On the contrary, tears of self-pity well in his eyes. He turns away as if he had been done an injustice. Even the reporter has overlooked the deeper meaning of the event, and adds, "...For he had many possessions" — for all the world as if he were offering an excuse! (Mark 10:22).

And finally we have Jesus' criticism of Martha. "Martha, Martha, how concerned and anxious you are about so many things! Actually, only one thing is necessary" (Luke 10:41). Here again we encounter the "one thing it's all about" — which Martha, bustling and distracted, constantly cooking or washing dishes, completely misses. Overextension with housework is a typical female escape. Housework is frequently busy work, and
√ when this is the case, then our preoccupation with it is only laziness and superficiality. Our real purpose is precisely to avoid the more profound, crucial task of becoming what we can become and what we therefore should be — the task of becoming ourselves, the task of individuation.

One day, as Jesus was journeying along the road, someone called out, "Let me come with you! Everywhere!" But Jesus said, "Foxes have their holes, birds have their nests, but the Son of Man has nowhere to lie down and rest" (Luke 9:57). Do you still want to come with me? Under these conditions? Jesus addresses this person's conscience implicitly, but powerfully.

Evidently he has discerned the superficial enthusiasm of a mere velleity. Hiding beneath the shrill assurances of consciousness is a deep, intimate, unconscious incapacity or unwillingness to change. Jesus examines people closely. Where harshness is justified, he is harsh.

In another instance it is Jesus, and not his addressee, who surmises a potential discipleship. Jesus calls to the man, but hears in reply: "Excuse me, I'd like to come — but first let me tell my family good-bye" (Luke 9:61). On the face of it, the request is surely a reasonable one. But Jesus must have sensed some typical, hidden resistance. Well, then, why don't we just drop it, Jesus responds. At least this is the meaning of Jesus' rejoinder in context. Of still another candidate, Jesus' premonition is reported explicitly. Ah, this might be a candidate. But the latter replies, "Please excuse me — I have to go to my father's funeral first." Jesus' response is one we should never dare speak out so forthrightly! "Let the dead bury their dead" (Luke 9:59–60) — we have more important things to do! Now — let us be honest — does that not sound unbearably harsh? To judge from the surface meaning of the words alone, is this not raw insensitivity? But we grasp those words in another light altogether, if the mourner was simply lying — to Jesus and to himself. In the Far East the idiom the man employs is a familiar one. In India I once met a gentleman who, as all his acquaintances knew, proposed to become a Christian once his father had passed away. Again and again he would be heard to say, "I must first bury my father." His deeper intent, however, was absolutely unconnected with a filial piety that would wish to spare a father the sight of a son's apostasy — however staunchly the son might believe that this was his motivation. Actually the protester was afraid he would be disinherited. The father died, but his place in the family unit was taken over by the elder brother. And our catechumen was back with his old excuse: "I must first bury my brother." But the brother outlived him. Decades of make-believe, of self-deception, were now fruitless. Altogether likely we have a similar case in the powerful New Testament passage before us. A psychological corrigendum would read: "First I must get my hands on my inheritance." In

Far and Near East alike, a patrimony enjoys the overpowering motivational primacy reserved by Freud for sex. And in any event it is easy to see that Jesus sensed the true character of his invitee's response. In view of the unconscious resistance of that response, Jesus' reaction is no longer at all surprising. He is simply reacting to the facts. And when we regard those facts in depth, his response is altogether appropriate.

These examples will suffice for our examination of the question with which we are concerned here: How does Jesus deal with unconscious or neurotic resistance? Our answer will be in three parts. First, Jesus *dis-covers* the resistance. He brings it out into the open, as far as it will come. We modern therapists approach this discovery, this uncovering, by employing the tools of an analytic depth psychology that we prize as a great twentieth-century discovery, as of course it is. Jesus was able to effectuate it on his own, with nothing beyond the tools of his own personality. This is the historical fact confronting us here.

Once the problem is uncovered, Jesus approaches it in a fashion calculated to *lead the sufferer to self-knowledge.* This is the only way the patient can be helped. Jesus pounds away at no one, compels no one, overwhelms no one. He will not try to talk you into anything. People call out, "Have pity on us! Help us if you can!" and Jesus answers, "That depends on you!" (Mark 9:23). That depends mostly on whether your basic attitude is a positive or a negative one — whether you not only very *much* want to be helped, but very *deeply,* as well.

Jesus does not attack the symptom. He strives for a *personal change* in the subject. The symptom will disappear of itself. The basic validity of this approach has been demonstrated by more than one scientific discipline. The reason we fail to see it in Jesus is that we overlook the breadth of Jesus' dynamics. As integrated, open human beings, we ought to be able to read the New Testament account of Jesus in a new way, and certainly without ignoring the findings of modern historical criticism.

In sum: Jesus responds to unconscious or neurotic resistance exactly, in principle, as modern therapists might only wish they were able to.

But what of those whom Jesus addresses? What might we

learn from the unconscious resistance of those whom Jesus confronts, whether they follow him or turn away? After all, we are not very different from people in those days. We see this once more from an analysis of dreams. What is the look of *unconscious resistance today?* Let us consider a few concise examples.

A teaching fellow had made a valiant struggle to succeed with her analysis. But suddenly she reported a dream of a very specific type. In her dream, I, her analyst, appeared as a sorceress, swathed in a copious silken mantle, wearing a turban of many colors, and holding in my hands an emerald shell, from which billows of marvellous incense tumbled in a blinding cloud. The room itself had the appearance of a mystic chapel. At once we have the suggestion of a wondrous, wholesale ravishing to some ethereal sphere. In the gospels, too, over and over again we hear the demand of the crowds for "signs and wonders" — when people ought to be asking what is being demanded of *them!* "A sure sign?" Jesus muses, in anger. "These people want proof? Well, they shall have nothing of the kind" (Mark 8:11–12). And what else could I tell the learned lady who had come to me? You see me as a sorceress because you want a miracle. You should know better than that. There will be no such thing. *You* must work. You must give up your resistance to the demands of your analysis.

A young theologian, in no condition to respond to the demands of analysis for the moment, reported the following dream. He had gone into a bookstore to use the telephone. He only wanted to call home, but "for propriety's sake," he told me, "I had to buy a book too. I asked where the paperback section was, thinking that I could get a cheap book there. The owner held his hands about a foot apart and told me that he only had 'this many' paperbacks. I went to the back of the store and there on my right, high on a shelf, I saw a great number of books. There was a volume by Jung among them, but it cost 78 marks. Besides, when I went to reach for it, it was too high for me. There were stools to stand on, though." Every sentence of the young gentleman's recital betrays resistance, and that resistance was unbreakable. For appearance' sake alone, he decides to buy a book. He heads straight for the inexpensive section of the bookstore. There he finds books of great value. But he "can't quite reach them." That is, he exerts no effort whatever. He sees the stools, he consciously adverts to their purpose, but we never hear that he climbed up on one. He wants everything at a discount — without effort. All is façade, all is "acting as if." Had Jesus asked him, "Do you want to be well?" he would have replied, "Yes!" — for appearance' sake. There is a superficiality that will dig in its heels at all cost, and this is the most stubborn resistance of all, in small affairs as in great, yesterday as today.

A very successful industrial engineer came to me with nervous insomnia. He had tried countless remedies, but all had failed. In analysis with me, he had the following dream. He heard a voice call, "Wake up, you!" Bristling at what seemed to him the height of unreasonableness, the dreamer shouted back, "No! I want to sleep! I don't want to wake up!" And indeed his insomnia turned out to be a somatic reveille addressed to his psyche — altogether appropriate, in view of his inner sleep. It appeared that he was shirking a great responsibility in his private life. He was offering far too little in the way of togetherness or partnership to a wife who loved him very much, and who was ill besides. His own pleasure always came first. Now his analysis seemed to really "take off." His dreams, his cooperation, surprised me. Then he made a drawing for me — straight out of the unconscious, without any preliminary sketches, but simply dashed off. And it coincided with a turning point. It showed a man under an apple tree. Reaching up toward the tree, which was laden with rich, ripe fruit, the man all but had an apple in his hand. The meaning of the drawing in the artist's conscious mind was to signal the end of his analysis, and indeed he soon came in with the customary flowers, book, and so on. He had laid the groundwork for his retreat. That is, he was backing out. The resistance that had been latent all along now came to light, sketched in a picture of a man with an apple almost in his hand. As his drawing revealed, my client had no wish to exert one last little effort that would have made the apple his. That would have meant accepting the demands of his analysis. He would have had to give up his selfishness. That would have been too hard. And we have an actual, graphic representation of unconscious resistance.

We have spoken of the individual conscious and unconscious resistance encountered by Jesus, and how he dealt with it so effectively. But what of the *collective resistance* mounted by the people, the resistance Jesus encountered in the people as a compact mass? The answer to this question lies in a completely different direction. Here we must deal with the collision of two completely incompatible psychological strata, incapable of reconciliation.

Even allowing for the impact on the texts of tendentious interpretation, we cannot escape the impression given in the gospel accounts that wherever Jesus appeared, whatever he said or did, he stirred a storm of disapproval and contradiction. His adversaries held their secret consultations, and as a last resort attempted to trap him in his speech through a series of sanctimonious questions. These problems became more and more compromising. Obviously the intent was not only to get something on him, but to set him up — to lay the groundwork for the fabrication of some evidence of capital crimes, or at least of such transgressions as would have entailed his exclusion from the religious community of his people. Here, resistance is not only dogged and vicious; it is lethal. "His opponents seethed with rage" (Luke 6:11).

The milieu in which Jesus moved was a rigid, consolidated, legalistic religious society. A religion of law had won dictatorial authority over absolutely everything, to life's least and most intimate details, from courtroom to kitchen. There was no place for Jesus in such a society, and the most up-to-date scholarship has demonstrated beyond any doubt whatsoever that Jesus himself became aware of this in short order. And by the time he entered Jerusalem, it was quite clear to him that he was not on his way to a solemn enthronement.

In his society, two thousand years ago, Jesus didn't stand a chance. Why not? Because he was a person who was absolutely *natural* in his thoughts and actions. No hairsplitting casuistry can abide such a deportment. It senses the loss of its security, its certitude. It feels threatened, and threatened to its very bones.

It has been called into question, and this in its very essence.

Jesus was *open to contact,* at every moment. For a religion of law this means strangulation. Suddenly high and low, pure and impure, permitted and forbidden, are not clear cut.

Jesus was *spontaneous,* in word and work. As a person who was open to contact, he could scarcely have been unspontaneous. But for a society frozen in rules, differentiating each and every separate thing to the tolerance of a hair's breadth — a society which therefore will never act spontaneously — this is a mortal sin. A legalistic society must everlastingly ask, as its prime concern: "Is it permitted ... ?" (Matt. 12:10) — and indeed this is the question it so typically and so often puts to Jesus.

Jesus was *consistent.* What he had seen as the right, or the truth, or the humane, he ached to see materialized in deed. This went without saying, be the one standing before him an ostracized sinner, a woman for stoning, a defenseless child, a pious hypocrite, or a self-righteous rabbi. But if there is one thing a religion of unadulterated legalism cannot abide, it is a consistent application of norms. Legalism will develop a fine-honed casuistry to determine what is appropriate in this case and what in that, what one does and what one does not do, what is plainly and simply permissible, what is only minimally permissible but still permissible, and what is simply impermissible — illegitimate. Jesus labeled a casuistry like that, a casuistry embracing the totality of life and suppressing the rights of the weak, the suffering, and the poor, as "hypocrisy," in so many words. And of course he was right.

Jesus was *totally committed.* He really saw the suffering individual who stood before him, although of course without ever losing sight of the people as a unity. His rational thinking could not prescind from the visceral offense of all that his keen perception brought to light. The most precious human rights, the most profound human duties, were being out and out trodden underfoot. A thoroughly detailed, differentiating religion of legalism, like that of Jesus' time and place, simply cannot stomach total commitment. Its hero is the ingenious compromiser, the one who can be depended on to come up with a new subterfuge for any occasion.[9]

Worst of all, as Herbert Braun has put it so beautifully in his remarks about the "authority Jesus won from his followers and hearers":

> He advocated and lived all the things about which we have already spoken. That gained him the hearts and minds of his hearers. They could not elude what he wanted. Whoever opposed what he wanted did it at the price of being unable to silence the inner voice that then said, but he *really* was right.[10]

For a totally elitist, arbitrary, patriarchal hierarchy of legalism, then, Jesus was a veritable walking, public reproach. That you couldn't stand for. That you got rid of.

There are times in the lives of individuals and peoples that we call moments of truth, hours of destiny. All of a sudden, fate itself steps forward and demands: "Decide. Which way now?" Jesus' appearance in his society was the inauguration, precious and rare, of just such a magnificent opportunity. That opportunity went unrecognized.

So much, then, for the attitude of the collectivity around Jesus. But what of *Jesus' attitude toward this collectivity?* It must have been possible for him to protect himself against this compact resistance. Yes, of course it was, and ways of doing so were arranged by his friends and even recommended to him. But Jesus kept faith with a basic principle of his: "You must hold out to the end to be saved" (Matt. 16:22–23, 10:22).

And so he held out to the end. Unwaveringly, even in a hopeless situation, he vindicated the *essential, basic truths of what it means to be a human being.* He defended these truths in their psychic, ethical, social, and metaphysical aspects. His advocacy of the essential truths of the psyche became, in and of itself, an act of decisive social relevance. Psychotherapy, with its advocacy of the essential basic truths of the psyche, acquires in and of itself a *social or societal relevance.* Psychotherapy today, by and large, is still a long way from having grasped this fact. *Jesus the therapist teaches us the urgency of this task.* The last thing Jesus he will do is fall back in the face of shattering collective antagonism.

The question he puts to the patient of Bethesda, then — "Do you want to be well?" — is invested not only with an individual reference, but with a socially comprehensive one as well. This is altogether evident. Within the four walls of the consultation room the scope of an analysis tends to be bounded by the interests of the individual. Should we manage to involve a rigid, defensive husband as well, or perhaps a whole family, we think we have really succeeded. Modern therapists are anything but a match for the destructive impact of the collective trend. Perhaps they are too much the prisoner of it themselves even to be aware of the problem.

And yet, never in all of history has a collective resistance to basic human truths been as generalized as we find it today. Anyone who has ever witnessed the misery of the "concentration henhouses" or *factory farms, with their bestial torture* of steers, calves, and now even lambs, knows the relentless, brutal violence done the individual and collective human psyche, entirely apart from the fact that a beast in human custody has a claim to humane treatment instead of brutal exploitation. Why do the defenders of the individual and collective psyche fail to rise up en bloc against this barbarity? After all, its consequences fall not only on the poor beasts, but on the human psyche as well, especially the collective psyche, and just as banefully. This psychic blindness, this rigidity, this cowardice, this concern with "not getting involved," is altogether unforgivable. Jesus — a therapist of another caliber — would scarcely have been so quiet.

A plethora of *ecological problems* stares our society in the face. Of course they are all the consequences of our decades-old exploitation and selfishness. Dead rivers and streams, dirty air, the dangers posed by nuclear technology, and so on, are just part of a long list of ecological tasks and challenges. To focus on just one problem: Why are the appointed guardians of the individual and collective psyche so silent in the face of the consumption by the millions, in Italy and elsewhere, of our larks and other songbirds?

Societies have been formed for the rescue of the ecological balance, and they are hard at work. But when I asked the president of the Jungian organization to bring the problem to the floor at the most recent congress of psychotherapists — to be held in Rome, as it happened — there was allegedly nothing, "to his regret," that he could do. And yet the Italian wildlife organizations were cheering me on with a mighty "Brava!"

Where was the voice of the therapists when the *abortion question* was being discussed? They, of all people, had abundant occasion to make themselves heard. Women are constantly coming to us with the typical abortion traumas and neuroses. (Of course, one must be able to recognize these. Their onset is not immediately after the abortion, but toward the moment when the birth would have occurred. That is when we hear, "Oh, if I had only realized!") And so we have an ongoing, legally protected, traumatization of the collective psyche. The universal psychic level is driven deeper and deeper into a collective neurosis of unsurmised dimensions. The consequences are ever with us. Why do we fail to oppose the causes? With the rare exception of a few insightful, courageous individuals, psychotherapy, at least for the moment, knows no prevention — only repair.

Jesus went to his death rather than yield to a neurotic collective resistance. *We have a hard lesson to learn from Jesus the therapist: not to accommodate to the collectivity in matters of injustice* — where human values are suffering harm — but rather to take responsible cognizance of the collective psyche and proceed accordingly.

Given the current level of our therapeutic consciousness, are we in anything like a position to learn this lesson?

Collective Resistance Today

But it is the present condition of societal consciousness that demands we subject the problem of collective resistance to one more brief but crucial examination. In the earlier pages of this chapter we observed that Jesus' question, "Do you want to be well?" is the vehicle of three very specific and challenging emphases. To "want" here, to will, means really to be willing to get moving. The importance of the "you" is that it must be I, and not someone else, who wills that I be well. Finally, "well" means completely well, and not merely free of a symptom. Once healed to the marrow, I may well expect my symptoms to be swept away in the flood of my new health.

But who in our society today is ready for this mighty a task? The whole thrust of our current culture consists in a down-levelling, a reduction, an easing, a softening, and of course with inexhaustible obligingness. But we are not saying that each and every person is being asked to achieve total integration, or individuation, or self-becoming. So brilliant an accomplishment is neither demanded nor expected of each and all. Often enough the urgent problem of the moment may be susceptible of a solution merely by way of a few steps in the right direction. But that is the point — the inescapable, ineluctable point. The steps must be in the right direction.

Even this seems too much to ask of today's collectivity. Instead of a few steps in the right direction, the modern seeker after mental health prefers a shortcut, especially a shortcut promising incredible benefits without an investment in terms of exertion. I refer to the phenomenon of group therapy.

Of necessity, I have become deeply involved with the problem of group therapy. I have had, and have, a series of patients in therapy who come away from their groups with severe psychic damage. I have had physicians in analysis whose prolonged contact with such groups, often in a leadership capacity, has left them so blocked, so numbed, so deprived of any inner flexibility that no analysis is even possible for the time being. It is as if their unconscious must first recover from shock.

Let me state very emphatically that I do not oppose groups as such. There have always been little Christian communities that for one reason or another we might call groups, from the house communities in New Testament times to such modern vehicles of community or congregational ministry as discussion groups, study groups, youth groups, pastoral groups, and so on. In the area of the natural sciences, including medicine, research work and the like has been carried on by societies, communities, and teams ever since the birth of science. I have nothing against the group that sticks to its last. Let me make that altogether clear once more. And it is a commonplace that each group develops a dynamic of its own, so that the group becomes more than the sum of its individual members. I first heard of the "dynamic of a community mentality" that a group develops from my philosophy teacher.

But I am definitely opposed to the group that does *not* stick to its last, claiming to replace or even improve on authentic psychotherapy, and with far less sweat along the way — promising, to boot, new, undreamed-of pots of gold at the end of the rainbow.[11]

In view of our subject, it will be in order to make mention of two works: *Group Counselling,* by J. W. Knowles, and the collection of essays appearing under the title *Gruppendynamik und kirchliche Praxis* ("Group Dynamics and Church Practice").[12] Both of these books are widely recommended for group work done under church auspices, and both are part of the series, *Praxis der Kirche heute* ("Church Practice Today"). But both are also symptomatic of the aims and the mentality of the groups in question, which, in their ebullient, free-swinging style, encourage their readership to discard "old ways" and adopt certain new methods. What transpires here is extolled as a genuine community of the Holy Spirit. The fact of the matter is that all steps in the right direction are avoided, and on principle. One knows better ways — the shortcuts to which we have referred — the more rapidly and fruitfully to achieve one's goal. Or so runs the frivolous promise. Even first steps in the right direction, beginner's steps, are declined. Both therapy manuals could well be retitled: "Collective Resistance Today."

Astonishingly, group discourse is all but preempted by the question of "style." Content, allegedly, presents no problem. For example, the ill success of church proclamation today is designated a "communication problem." It should be an a priori evidence that such an assessment is as naive as it is false. The real problem, of course, lies not in style, but in content. The problem is the "what," not the "how." Not so, however, in the mind of the devotees of group therapy. And so naturally the be-all becomes the "transmittal of new techniques." One pursues "new attitudes and behaviors," or "new structures" — always prescinding from the actual matter at hand. We hear of "transactions," "interactions," and "coping." But then sud-

denly we hear of "therapeutic methods." Now we are in different waters altogether, as the titles of the works cited give us to
surmise. Next it even comes to the interpretation of dreams,
and now we know that we are dealing with the most blatant
nonsense. Our groups deal with "projections" and attempt to
clear up "externalizations." They manage "transference" and
eradicate "counter-transference." Our criticism here is not our
"therapists'" imprecise grasp of the meaning or content of these
technical terms. The real problem is that persons without the
slightest notion of the dynamics of the unconscious plainly hold
themselves forth as being in a position to manage the most central problems of analytic theory. Analysis is not even listed
among the requirements for a group leader.

The problems addressed in the terminology just cited refer
wholly and entirely to events of the unconscious psyche. They
can therefore be dealt with only if one can seize upon that unconscious, as it were, comprehend its information, and draw the
corresponding practical consequences. *This* sort of group work,
then, is not medicine, but the amateurism of the dilettante.

We hear, moreover, that not only shall we progress more
rapidly under the auspices of a group than, say, in analytic
therapy — but that, unlike the latter (which from time to time
comes in for reduction to smithereens by the use of the epithet
"professional"), the new, group approach will "involve the whole
person." Our self-styled therapists are obviously innocent of
the faintest surmise that by far the greater part of the "whole
person" — to stay with the same quantitative model, despite its
inadequacy — is constituted by the unconscious.

In terms of the evolution of human consciousness, the group
activity under consideration represents a grave collective regression. Where ethos is concerned, its name here is insincerity.
Promises impossible to keep are made nonetheless. As for the
phenomenon itself, it would be fair to call it quackery.

Jesus, too, came in contact not only with individuals, but
with groups, large and small, that boasted they could guide
people to self-awareness, righteousness, and salvation, but that
lacked any qualifications for such a role. Jesus calls them the
"blind leading the blind." He asks: "Can one blind person show

another where the road is? Won't both of them fall in the ditch?" (Matt. 15:14, Luke 6:39).

And yet our new-style groups would lead us to our goal with the least possible effort on our part. On the one hand they all say: Look at us! *We're* well, aren't we? Then surely we can help you as well. Of course, the way shown to us must not be too exerting. It requires no effort to shriek obscene words over and over, as in scream therapy. Your face may be as red as a beet, but you certainly are not working hard. Screaming requires about as much effort as sinking into someone's comforting embrace, as in an encounter group. Jesus' question is, "Do you want to be well?" The group answer is, "Yes, but...." In other words, no.

Group therapy in our present sense has become dangerously widespread. It represents a very particular phenomenon. It sets up an *organized collective resistance* to Jesus' question. When all is said and done, our highest goal is only to be "accepted." What is actually fostered, with all of this group stroking, embracing, and sentimentality, is infantilism and neuroses. In this situation, like a fist banging on a table, Jesus' question brings us back to reality: "Do you want to be well?"

Justifiable Resistance

It is the will that counts, declares our chapter title — a will that will brook no resistance. We have spoken of conscious, unconscious, and collective resistance. Now let us introduce another concept. Precisely in a context of the therapy practiced by Jesus himself, let us consider the psychic phenomenon of *justifiable resistance.* Here is a concept all but entirely unknown to psychotherapy today. There is a resistance to the analyst that is legitimate and justified, and we may learn of it from the history of Jesus the therapist. As we have seen, Jesus' therapy is first and foremost a spontaneous function of the therapist as a person. Now, even justifiable resistance is a phenomenon of the unconscious. Consciousness continues to protest: Oh, I'll make it! — while the unconscious has been saying all along: No, you won't, and you'd better not try.

Let us begin with today's practice, and give Jesus the final word in this chapter as we did in the last.

My client came to me a broken person. Her greatest difficulty did not consist in personal problems. Rather, when she had sought help for them, the analyst to whom she had applied had taken it upon himself to certify her as unsuitable for therapeutic treatment with, "My, you are completely dead inside!" This was a terrible thing for her to have to hear. After a great deal of hesitation, she broke off the analysis. Was her resistance justified?

We cannot dissect such a case any further. We can only ask questions. Any inadequacy in the therapist has been brought on by himself, and is available to him alone for examination. His "self-transparency" is his alone. It is only in the measure of your own dynamic self-realization that you will find yourself "in the truth," and it is only in virtue of your own truth that you will be able to lead others to truth. Now, then, what is to be said of the dynamic self-transparency of my patient's former analyst?

The therapeutic school conventionally designated "psychoanalysis" has made a methodological virtue of the analyst's maximal reserve, decreeing that the analyst discharge his or her role, ideally at least, in all but cryptic anonymity. Let us understand our terms here. "Psychoanalysis" is the name generally reserved for the analysis developed by Sigmund Freud, or that of any school tracing its lineage exclusively to him. Other analytical approaches go by other names. Jung, for example, calls his method "analytical psychology." Speaking for myself, I can only say that, over the course of my years of practice, I have treated so many severely traumatized refugees from orthodox Freudian analysis that, while I continue to revere Freud as a great pioneer and an equally great genius, I regard analysts who emphasize the Freudian authenticity of their practice as, oftentimes, a real menace.

For example, August Kekule von Stradonitz, discoverer of the six-carbon benzene ring, attributed his discovery to a dream he had had of a serpent biting its tail while spinning in a circle. But when an Alexander Mitscherlich comes to examine Kekule's dream, the only conclusions he can draw would have been just as readily available from an orthodox analysis of a romance novel from the racks at the grocery checkout.[13] Thus we read of "the sex-wish numeral ... repression ... extreme love repression," and so forth and so on. We learn nothing that Freud and his successors had not long since explained to us. The only new element is the grotesque distortion of Kekule's dream. But that there might be a "discovery of truth" in the dream is "surely in error." We are privy, however, to no grounds the author might have for his pontifical assertion to this effect. That the structure of the benzene molecule could actually have been read from this dream is sheerly impossible — "a pure coincidence"!

What have we here? We have fantasy, unfounded dictatorial assertions, hypotheses, and dogmatism masquerading as science. Mitscherlich has good reason to "mourn"! He can mourn his ignorance of the creative function of the unconscious. He can mourn his ignorance of the collective unconscious. Both are discoveries of hoary vintage. He can mourn the shrivelled image of the human being he offers in the name of a poor positivistic, materialistic, naturalistic science. Further, this approach to analysis constantly introduces a corrosive positivism into the general thinking. Where is the requisite self-transparency here?

It is altogether understandable, then, that a Wolfgang Kretschmer should arrive at the following opinion:

> Of all currents in psychotherapy, psychoanalysis is the least suitable to function as the platform for a universal synthesis of theories and experiences. On the contrary: paradoxically, useful psychoanalytic perceptions can be retained only if one leaves psychoanalysis for greener pastures.... [14]

Why so? Precisely because of the imprisonment of psychoanalysis in theory, with its utterly impoverished picture of the human being.

If this is the state of affairs with the green wood, how will it be with the dry? It is of the utmost importance that we be clear in our own minds about one fact: by no means all of the resistance that crops up in analysis is to be laid to the account of the analysand. Modern depth psychology goes its happy, naive way, blissfully ignorant of this. Jesus the therapist, however, is emphatic on this point, and obviously with reason. Indeed, among the lessons we can learn from Jesus here is his *specific contribution* to the whole question. His warning concerning the "blind leading the blind" is forthright, as we have shown. And indeed, can one blind person guide another? (Matt. 15:14, Luke 6:39). Was the analyst in the following case not blind? Yet did he not attempt to guide someone into the light?

A student with a long history of analysis came to me for treatment. He had lain on his therapist's couch and talked, and talked and talked, until at last he had really nothing left to say. He had expressed himself without assistance: his analyst had done all the listening. "Sincerely, nothing else occurred to me!" he told me. And now the analyst and his client had sat for hours without a word. The young man reached the limit of his endurance. Then he hit upon a subterfuge. He had chanced upon a relatively unknown, but solid enough, work in psychology. He excerpted passages from the book, digested them in his own words, and conveyed them to his analyst as spontaneous material. The therapist's heart leapt for joy. Everything was all right after all. The analysis was on its way again. But the student was unable to stomach his ruse for long, and he finally broke off the analysis — an analysis that had gone on for years. Was his resistance justifiable?

Difficult as it may be to excuse the analysand's imposture, the analyst's failure to see through it, and to do so at once, boggles the mind. Furthermore, to drill to the bottom of the prehistory of the case, as he did, is completely unnecessary. This is one of the reasons some analyses go on forever. No, we should turn as quickly as possible to the information offered by the unconscious, to dreams, and to an understanding of those dreams. Anything germane in the patient's history will come *relentlessly* to light in the process. We hear of the autonomy of the unconscious. Rarely, however, do we find an analyst willing to place a great deal of trust in that autonomy. Instead, facile, handy theories are the order of the day.

I was burned once myself. Very early in my studies I entered analysis with a renowned analyst. A shingle over the sidewalk trumpeted her specialty: *Die gesamte Psychotherapie*—all psychotherapy, no less. Had I known then about depth psychology what I know now, of course, I should have turned on my heel the moment I read the sign. But I began my analysis. After some few hours I had the following dream to report. I dreamed I had left two small articles of clothing at the laundry and had come back to pick them up. A lady handed them to me along with a bill for twenty-some marks. "That's a lot of money for a little laundry," I thought to myself in my dream. My analyst asked me for my free association. I had to admit I thought of the analysis. In fact the laundry bill amounted to the cost of an analysis session at that time. Then I had another dream. I dreamed that I had a great appetite for a nice, juicy piece of ham and that I had gone to a butcher shop to buy some. Well, there was ham, all right, but only a gray old end-slice. And I left the shop in disappointment. Once more my free association bore on the analysis. "Old ham," of course, expressed a resistance fairly screaming to be taken seriously. A third dream followed. The general import was the same. I was hungry. I wanted some fresh, nutritious whole-grain bread. But the only bread in the bakery was white — soft and spongy. I left the shop. To my chagrin I had to report a free association bearing once more on my analysis. Then came a fourth dream. This one was wall-to-wall archetypal symbols and similarly charged expressions. One could almost have said that, after first trying a couple of gentle, almost humorous hints in the form of the previous intimations, the unconscious had finally slammed its fist down on the table. The analyst just sat there helplessly. She had absolutely nothing to say about the dream. Not for a moment did it occur to her that there could be something amiss in her procedure. Of course this was precisely where the dream pointed. But she could only suggest I consult another analyst — and promptly made certain I sensed how little her recommendation was the function of her undiluted benevolence toward my person.

I have never experienced another episode like that. I have found understanding analysts both in Germany and abroad. But thanks to this initiation, I have always exercised the greatest caution not to practice analysis on the exclusive basis of authority or of some fixed schemata. Indeed, it was the narrow, rape-like approach of that rigid Freudian analyst that my unconscious had been protesting against in those bygone days. When an analysand manifests symptoms of resistance, one of the first things I ask myself, as a matter of principle, is: Could it possibly — just possibly — be justified? And in my opinion all analysts should ask themselves this same question, over and over again. Had they always done so, things would never have come, for example, to the following pass.

A university professor terminated his analysis with a female therapist. "What interesting dream material you have!" the latter had frequently remarked. But eventually — as he later recounted to me, resuming his analysis — a certain uneasiness stole over him, and he found it more and more difficult to suppress it. The analyst, who was not married, "seemed for all the world to be trying to drive a wedge between me and my wife with her interpretations." Finally the client expressed his discomfort a number of times, only to be reproached for introducing "tensions" into his analysis. At this the professor, who, as it happened had actually lectured on depth psychology, was perceptive enough to inquire: "But where is any of this in my dreams? How do my dreams suggest this?"

The analysis ended with a "bang." Now the client dreamed that he was playing a dramatic role on stage. In the course of the development of the plot he was to strike his head, as if it had suddenly come home to him that he had committed some great error, or that he was guilty of a particular piece of stupidity. Simultaneously there was to be a loud report in the theater. Bang! All went as planned. But when the play was at an end, the dreamer criticized the bang to the producer and director. They waxed indignant. "What? Just that one 'bang' cost us twelve thousand marks!" Our analysand reported his dream to his analyst and remarked that he had just gone over his accounts and calculated that the remainder of his analysis would cost twelve thousand marks. That was the "tally." Blazing indignation. Of course the pair, to the accompaniment of the standard forced signs of politeness, agreed that another "discussion session" was in order. But the last word was the analyst's: "*I shall never* [!] *admit* that this dream bears on the analysis!" And of course this was precisely the problem. Innumerable analysts would speak exactly in the same way. They have never — never — allowed themselves a glimpse of justifiable resistance, and therefore will never admit its existence. "I shall never admit" is the language of the blind leading the blind.

From time immemorial, physicians have been succor and salvation to those who invoke them. In their hands, only too often, has lain life and death. As a consequence they have been wreathed in the aura of a numinous authority. Indeed, in the Old Testament God is symbolized in the image of the physician: "I am the Lord your physician" (Exod. 15:26). Therapists frequently appear in their patients' dreams as some powerful magician, cunning sorcerer, or trickster at whose prowess and agility one can only gasp in wonder. Such dream symbols are problematic in the extreme, of course. That last bastion of Western superstition, then, that divine medicine, hoary psychotherapy, must suffer the divestiture of its ageless hypostatization. Agonizing as some of the accompanying phenomena may be, this simply *must* come to pass. Patients must achieve *independence* of the therapist. They must be told, "Keep nothing back. Suppress nothing. When you feel antagonism and opposition, come right out with it." We *all* occasionally encounter justifiable antagonism and opposition. To seek to dispute this principle is to bestow upon the rank of physician (here, of psychotherapists) the attribute of absolute perfection. But we must admit that such perfection is not ours. This avowal is an essential component of the self-transparency or self-discernment required of the therapist. Moreover, if the therapist has taken a false step, a protest will be registered on the part of the unconscious, especially in the ensuing dreams. The unconscious goes its *own* way to the reestablishment of the psychic equilibrium. Of course, if these forthright corrective expressions are thereupon misinterpreted, a still more profound neurotic disorientation will result, and one had better see another analyst.

What about Jesus here? Jesus was always open to the possibility of justifiable resistance. We hear precious little of this in

conventional religious circles. Apart from New Testament scholarship, Christians nearly always begin with a dogmatic picture
of Jesus. We expect each and every deed and utterance to be
absolute. After all, are these words and these actions not special, wondrous threads in the great tapestry of God's salvation
plan? But now we have our mind so exclusively on what God
is thinking and planning that we completely overlook what the
New Testament says. No wonder, then, that modern citizens
of a culture that has dogmatized the data of revelation beyond
recognition for millennia typically feel so little attraction for the
church or dogma, and more and more for the figure of Jesus.

First, then, we may observe that Jesus is at every moment
prepared to agree with his interlocutor, whatever his own initial
intentions. By way of example we need cite only the account
of the centurion at Capernaum. The latter voices his desire
concerning his sick servant. Jesus replies: "I shall come." But
a home visit is not what the centurion has in mind. "I do
not deserve that honor," he says. Whereupon Jesus, instead of
proceeding on the principle, "This is what I have decided, and
this is how it shall be," is impressed by the centurion's ensuing
explanation and cancels plans for the home visit. "Let it happen
as you believe" (Matt. 8:5–13). To objections, suggestions, or
justified questions Jesus is open, pliable, and flexible.

I know of only one instance in which Jesus encounters appropriate, justified, deep resistance — namely, the case of the foreigner from Phoenicia, who intercedes on behalf of her daughter
who is ill (Matt. 15:21–28, Mark 7:24–30). At first Jesus is unwilling to accede to her request. And we hear the hard words
about throwing children's bread to dogs. But the Phoenician
is a quick-witted interlocutor. Her desire, her sick daughter, is
much too important to her. "But at least dogs get what children toss under the table!" The literary account has suppressed
something here: Jesus experienced an inner human growth and
development — "obviously," we should add today. Jesus at first
believes that his mission is only to the twelve tribes of Israel.
Only gradually does his particularism yield to a sublime universalism. Scholarship recognizes and acknowledges this today. In
Jesus' conversation with the eloquent woman from Phoenicia,

we are privy to a giant forward step in his development. His response to her parry is pregnant with meaning: Now you have me. With this utterance Jesus testifies to an enormous change in himself. He has gained a new perception of his total existence, his total task.

How, then, does Jesus react to justifiable resistance? *He yields to it. He does justice to it. He learns from it himself. He actually allows himself to be called in question! And thereby he offers an excellent example to be followed by any psychotherapy, and any psychotherapist.*

Chapter 3

The Courage for Self-Encounter

Why all this resistance to an opportunity to be well? Because the neurotic is unwilling to give up what his or her neurosis bestows: the pursuit of pleasure and a position of power. This was Freud's answer, and we have concurred. But we must delve into some of the implications of the answer. How does the neurotic manage to adopt and maintain this inner attitude? Can it really be that the sufferer simply never grasps the horrendous selfishness that lies at the basis of any neurosis? Yes, precisely. The neurotic simply never lets things get that far. He or she has fallen victim to a psychic motivation that guides its subject blissfully to lay all guilt to the account of others, so that the sick person only gleams with the sheerest innocence. This inner, compulsive motivation (which is far from being the monopoly of the neurotic, as it happens), which finds its own deficit not with itself, basically, but with its neighbor, and unloads its guilt on that neighbor regardless of the actual state of affairs, is called projection. Jesus understood a great deal about projection. In fact, he understood everything basic to this psychic phenomenon. In the parable of the Pharisee and the tax collector, he has favored us with a graphic depth-psychology paradigm of this compulsive motivation.

Pharisee and Tax Collector

The parable itself (Luke 18:9–14) is known all over the world, even in non-Christian religions. It represents a turning point and permanent orientation in the history of religion and spirituality, sounding the death-knell of the "religion of exploits" — religion performing an impressive list of good works in order to "get in the clear" with God. In India the parable is reckoned among the Great Words: a sacred utterance, precious and rare.

The Pharisee "goes into the temple to pray." Of course, he does not pray; he makes a speech, and a carefully composed one. The orator is making his report to God. He omits nothing from the list of duties to be performed by a just and pious man, and includes a bit of supererogation to boot. Our man is a model of piety. We should also note that, although ultimately the Pharisee is the negative figure in the parable, Jesus assigns him no negative traits. There is no boasting here, no swaggering. Jesus is simply sketching a model of piety — a person who has actually done, really observed, everything that God has communicated. He prays "within himself," and here indeed is a person who lives within himself. He does not so much as wait for a response to his prayer, but gives it himself. We read it between the lines of every sentence of his report, as it grows in clarity and plainness until it is finally unmistakable to anyone: What a fine fellow! What a truly, genuinely pious man! Nor would anyone in all the community have in the least begrudged him his comparative reflection on the tax collector. How could anyone have censured it or been disturbed by it? After all, these tax-gougers were only too well known. Cheaters and embezzlers, they were. And they could be cruel, too.

Certain standard prayers had been handed down as a guide for thanking God — including, of course, thanking God that we were not born a woman. And our Pharisee pronounces just such a prayer, with an occasional flourish into the bargain.

Neither, let us note, does Jesus attribute any eminent qualities to the tax collector, even though the latter is to be the positive figure in the story. He may have been just as evil, for all we know, as any of the rest of his ilk. We should be ill advised to permit ourselves to imagine the Pharisee in a black hat and the tax collector in a white one. And yet they divide the world in two. How? Why? They certainly are not dead and gone. We are not dealing with forgotten personages of a a remote, meaningless past. No, the Pharisee and the tax collector are living, plastic symbols of the greatest currency. It would be no exaggeration to say, from the standpoint of depth psychology, that they are alive and well in the psyches of all times.

Shadow Projection

With the Pharisee it is not this or that particular quality that is to be abominated. It is everything, the whole man and his whole attitude. He moves in the sight of his God "with saucy matter-of-factness." Truly he stands atop a "mountain of conceit."[1] He imagines that his good works make everything all right, that he is in God's grace beyond the shadow of a doubt, and that consequently he has every right to look down on creatures like "this tax collector here." He has *so* much to show! Only one thing is missing: the courage for self-encounter. His repeated "I" is the formula of self-exaltation. When it comes to getting personal — he prefers to point to the tax collector standing behind him. The courage for self-encounter? He hasn't got a whit of it.

And this is the nub of the problem. So many people come for therapy with an urgent desire to be helped. Why, then, after a first few steps, do we so often encounter the resistance of which we have spoken? Because of a lack of will, we have answered. Now we may make our answer more specific: because the courage for self-encounter is lacking. Self-encounter, in terms of depth psychology, means encounter with, having it out with, one's "shadow." What is our shadow? It is by no means simply our evil side. Rather it consists of material that we have allowed to drift from view, material that we have forgotten, or "sat on." It is painful, and so it has been repressed. But it is also the nonexperienced — that which, despite the presence of the adequate apparatus, has never "materialized." In short, the shadow is the dark side of the personality. It is dark in that, instead of basking in the full light of consciousness, it lurks on the periphery, on the outer edge of that light. The shadow is a phenomenon of the penumbra. As it loses itself in the unconscious, however, it continues to be active. Gradually withdrawing from the control of the critical, lucid, responsible consciousness, it is an ideal nesting place for material that may happen to be less worthy, deviant, or out and out wicked. Thus the shadow can indeed stand for the ethically negative side of the personality as well.

By the very fact that the shadow is identical with psychic phenomena that do not lie within the orbit of the critical consciousness, obviously it will constitute an element of the unconscious. Now, the unconscious is really unconscious: we are unaware of it. But it is anything but inactive. On the contrary, the unconscious psyche is dynamically active. Since, then, the shadow is unconscious as far as the naive attitude of consciousness is concerned — wholly excluded from consciousness properly so-called, ostracized and repelled — it directs its activity without. It directs its activity against "the others." The Pharisee has a shadow. Indeed, his whole person comes on the scene as a self-righteous shadow figure. But even Jesus acknowledged a shadow. How else could we have the account of the temptation in the wilderness? And then we have the far more certain and direct evidence of his own emphatic refusal to be labeled a "good" teacher or master. No, he says, no one is good but God. "Good" is an absolute, totalizing concept. Metaphysically and ethically, at least, the comparative and the superlative of the adjective "good" indicate, not a greater good, but a lesser good than the simple, absolute good of the positive degree. Anyone who would presume to discourse upon the human Jesus must take note of this fact. Otherwise we shall have a mere dogmatic chimera. For there is no concrete human being without a shadow. Van der Leeuw, working from an analysis of the phenomena of religious history, summarizes as follows: The shadow "is necessary to life, if indeed it is not life itself." Only demons and the dead "lack shadows, both for Dante and among Central African negroes. . . . Fear of losing one's shadow is widespread."[2]

To own up to one's shadow takes courage. There may be

pain, and shame, in store! And so, from time immemorial, the
fear of the shadow prevails. Even Plato, in the *Phaedo,* and
Cicero speak of "being afraid of one's own shadow." In 1532
a certain *Anonymous Collection* appeared among the peoples
of German-speaking lands. One of its maxims read: " 'Afraid
of his own shadow' — said of a faint-hearted person."[3] Surely
not all of the implications available to depth psychology are
consciously present in this early reflection. And yet the line is a
therapeutic prize. For it is these "faint-hearted" who so readily
exclaim, "Oh, what's the use, anyway?"

It is fear of one's own shadow, then, the unwillingness to face
one's own deep insincerity, that issues in projection. Thus, *to
project means unconsciously to transfer one's own unconscious
to other persons, places, or things.*

The Pharisee projects his shadow onto the tax collector, and
obtains relief. Now his sense of security and well-being is en-
hanced in so many respects. We all know what the "black sheep
of the family" is: the whipping boy, who "naturally" has botched
everything up again. ("What did you expect?") In other words,
all of the other family members cast their shadows on this one
projection figure. Typically it is some weakness or handicap that
transforms this projection figure into a whipping boy. Incidentally, the term has only recently been reduced to a mere figure of
speech. There were actual whipping boys in Spain as recently as
the nineteenth century. From France, too, and especially from
England, we have frequent documentation of this barbaric cus-
tom. In fact, the German word *Prügelknabe* is only a literal
translation of the English "whipping boy." Whipping boys were
those unfortunate young pages, servants and companions of a
young prince, who, when the latter committed a transgression,
took the strokes of the lash on their own backs. This was a
truly concretizing shadow projection. The practice is likewise
reported in German cultural history, in connection with King
Konrad IV (1228–54), father of the last Hohenstaufen, Kon-
dradin, although it is recounted that Konrad vehemently and
perceptively protested the abuse.[4]

Projection figures, with all of their hopeless, innocent suffering, include not only individuals, but collectivities, of every

sort and milieu. In a nominal democracy — one that in actuality is a dictatorship of one or more political parties — an opposition party becomes the target of the diabolical, undiscriminating projection of all of the defects of the party in power. This projection, which is effectuated as dramatically and persuasively as possible, provides the party in power with security. But the classic projection figures have ever been the Jews, with their centuries-long history of the pogroms and now the politics of the annihilation of the state of Israel. The Armenians were whipping boys, as are the untouchable *panchamas* of India. The church projected its shadow in the Inquisition. Any adequate survey of the history of shadow projection would sweep us away in a veritable flood of examples. The shadow figure par excellence is still the black or, for that matter, any nonwhite. That this figure still functions is evinced in current racist policies in various parts of the world. The black has become so deep and so typical a shadow figure for our psyches today that our shadow still represents itself in dreams as a black person. Where objectivity fails, shadow projection prevails. Unelucidated, questionable, utterly subjective motives shift from the subject to the object. And as objectivity is rare, projection is the rule. Finally, collective shadow projections are verified today in the concept of *Feindbilder,* or model enemies.

It is more and more against this age-old background of subjective and collective projection that today's psyche functions. We who style ourselves "modern" of course keep no more physical, literal whipping boys. But let us not deceive ourselves as to the violent, barbaric inner state of our souls. Of course we have our whipping boys, and whipping girls! Only, we proceed with more discretion and refinement. After all, one must regard appearances. Our method is psychological. When analysis uncovers such a projection process actually under way, however, it will not be the faint-hearted or "those of little faith" who will have the wherewithal to face their shadow. "Comfort the faint-hearted" (1 Thess. 5:14), our post-Paschal tradition admonishes. To be sure. But their authentic comfort will consist in helping them uncover their shadow, cut off their projection, and thus extricate themselves from the lie they are living.

How does this process present itself in psychotherapy today?

In the middle of the night, the telephone rings. Gasping, a woman in treatment reports that she has been "completely devastated" by a dream. In her analysis, problems with her extended family have been playing an important role. The relatives are all "good for nothing." Now, in her dream, the analysand is standing on the balcony of her house, leaning on the wrought-iron railing and looking down on the relatives gathered in the yard. Suddenly something terrible happens. The railing snaps from its concrete mooring and the patient starts to tumble toward the yard. But at the last moment a hand catches her from behind and holds her. And my patient asks what I would have to say to all of this. The opening words of the pericope guiding our considerations present the parable of the Pharisee and the publican as a "story for such as regard themselves as estimable persons and look down on others" (Luke 18:9). And our analysand has literally used the expression, "I was looking down on them. . . . " This is how we see today's Pharisee dealing with everyday relationships. Actually, with her own rather juicy past, the analysand had not the slightest grounds for "looking down" on her relatives. But she held to her imagined moral superiority like a wrought-iron railing, and with iron determination. Asked what I should say to all of this, I replied: "Nothing better could have happened to you." And as a matter of fact the emotional devastation occasioned by this dream resulted in a psychic concussion that marked a turning point in the analytic process.

"If only it weren't for his mother," a woman explained, all in a tither. The mother-in-law was to blame for everything. Otherwise my client's marriage would have been all right. Her complaints were strident, and she brooked no contradiction. I asked to see her husband. I was astonished. Here was an altogether reasonable, cultivated gentleman, and I learned that *his* mother lived so far away that she rarely even came to visit, while the *wife's* mother lived practically next door. And now I heard the whole list of complaints all over again, but this time they were directed toward the appropriate individual, instead of being projected. The wife suffered such a powerful mother attachment that, pharisaically protecting her own mother, she projected the whole set of problems onto someone else. It is of the essence of blind or unconscious projection that the subject really believe the whole tissue of deceit that he or she is spinning. And this was the case with our distraught wife.

"My wife isolates me from everyone," the young husband complained. "Any time we're invited out she manages to get off just the right sort of remark so that we won't get invited back." And so on. I saw the young wife. "The problem is," she began, "my husband isolates me from everybody." And by way of substantiation I heard the same expressions, the same words, that I had already heard from the husband. This is typical of the tone of many marriages. The blame has been volleyed back and forth until the antipathy has become ingrained and ritualized. Both partners are Pharisees, as in the case of this particular couple.

The courtiers of old were certainly not "nice" to their whipping boys. They were barbaric with them, in keeping with the mores of the time. But psychotherapy teaches us, based on facts, that the shadow projecting, domineering person proceeds no more gently today. Shadow projection must bear a very considerable share of the blame for today's high suicide rate, for the conflict, the hatred, the rejection, the enmity, the disowning, that grinds down members of immediate families, extended families, and society at large. It shatters marriages and clogs the courts. Over the long term, shadow projection has a devastating effect on the psyche, as on life itself. Projections lash out blindly. When one fails to "retract" them, as we say in technical language, by means of a "differentiated consciousness" — that is, when one fails to clarify them objectively — they are dangerous in the extreme.

Mote and Beam

No one has the right to depreciate another human being in his or her humanity. This is the authentic liberalism inherent in Jesus' admonition, "Judge not, that you may not be judged" (Matt. 7:1). Jesus' words merit particular attention. The notion

that one should not ascribe one's own shortcomings to others
pervades the New Testament tradition; but the fundamental,
absolute injunction against disparaging, degrading, or judging
one's fellow human beings comes from Jesus himself. In fact,
it is integral to his commandment to love our neighbor, and
even — the command that is uniquely Jesus' — our enemy. It is
an integral part of his very concept of neighbor. Jesus means: I
have no right to judge another. You stand or fall on your own,
and this applies to everyone. Self-encounter is the exclusive
prerogative of the one concerned, and I have no more right to
blunder into the case than does any other precipitant, uninvited
judge. The principle, "Judge not, that you may not be judged,"
is generally understood in much too narrowly moralistic a sense,
as if it were a matter of not bringing deserved retribution down
on one's own head. In actuality, it establishes the *individual
right to unobstructed self-encounter*. The personal right to self-
encounter is therefore not a weight or burden, but a duty in
virtue of being a unique prerogative.

Who do you think you are, injuring your fellow human beings
in this way? By what right do you impose on them arbitrary
burdens that would not even exist but for your own impotence?
How dare you? This is the tone of Jesus' familiar admonition
concerning the speck and the plank: "Why do you stare that
way at the speck in your brother's eye, and not even notice the
plank in your own eye? How dare you say to your brother,
'Come here a minute, let me take that speck out of your eye,'
when your own eye has a whole plank in it? You strutter! You
performer! You even fool yourself! First get rid of that plank
before you make a fuss about the speck in your brother's eye"
(Matt. 7:3–5). How dare you, you judger of specks?

The basic prohibition against unwarranted interference with
the person of others, on the grounds that we all stand or fall on
our own before God and our fellow human beings, is also emphasized in the pericope on the speck and the plank. And we
should be perfectly clear about it. Jesus is saying: you have *no
moral right whatsoever* to do what you are doing. Who is worse
off, anyway, you with your plank, or your neighbor with that
little speck? The plank represents a ponderous shadow, mas-

sive and menacing. It can be lethal. Jesus is absolutely right, and from the viewpoint of depth psychology this is a matter of principle: all speck-judgers are precisely persons who go about burdened with a shadow as heavy and ungainly as a plank or beam. People don't go around judging specks unless they have a plank for a shadow. The image of the plank underscores not only the gravity of the matter, and the danger involved, but the dimensions of the injustice as well.

In sum: Jesus has penetrated projection to the core. This is a key element in his therapy, and we are not surprised to find evidence of this in many another scriptural locus. His tone is: Self-encounter is a God-given *basic right,* to which one *may and must* correspond. As a privilege of the highest order, it is an obligation, as well. To hinder anyone in the exercise of this privilege and the discharge of this obligation through violent projection issuing in constant, active interference betrays a basic deficiency, a *perverted humanity,* in the one doing the projecting. For Jesus, projection is an all-around injustice, psychological, moral, and religious. Jesus alone has ascribed to the problem this sort of *universality.*

Shadow Encounter as Conversion Experience

The courage for self-encounter is crucial. Self-encounter is ineluctably the recognition and the acknowledgment of one's own shadow. It means seeing oneself as one really is. Shadow dreams are typical in the opening stages of an analysis. We must uncover, and as far as possible shake off, everything inauthentic and self-conceited, everything arrogant and presumptuous. Then we may proceed to deal with the genuine human being.

Now, what about our tax collector? The Pharisee's prayer is as lengthy as it is devoid of content. The tax collector's prayer, on the contrary, is short and charged with content. The tax collector only strikes his breast and says, "God, be lenient with me. I am a bad person." He stands in a place where he will be all but unnoticed, and he hardly dares look up. But "as he returned home, his fault was forgiven him" (Luke 18:13–14). Why? Because he had seen his tax collector's shadow and

had acknowledged it as his own. Thereby he had experienced
a genuine self-encounter — that infallible gateway to true development.

And this is the mystery surrounding the figure of Jesus. Jesus automatically, as it were, confronts his interlocutor with his
or her shadow. The centurion of Capernaum is a soldier. He
will not be precisely a paragon of delicacy. And he is a captain.
He will be sensitive about his rank, and the respect he thinks
he deserves. Then why does he say: Oh, no, don't come to my
house, I don't deserve the honor! (Matt. 8:5–13). He had not
stood before Jesus a moment before he knew Jesus' worth. Has
anyone else in history had this effect on people?

Zacchaeus! Who thinks anything of him? Jesus does, and
his "I'll be over today!" (Luke 19:1–10) is enough to convert his
thrilled addressee — the whole man. Zacchaeus acknowledges
his shadow, and makes restitution for all his injustice besides.
Jesus not only teaches the courage for self-encounter, he creates
it. He fairly radiates it, in all its dynamic power.

The woman known all over town, the one they called the
great sinner, drew looks of scorn as she dared to bathe Jesus' feet
with her tears, dry them with her hair, and anoint them (Luke
7:36–50). But Jesus let her do as she pleased, fully conscious of
the general disapproval of the company. Never had this person
bowed lower. But never, as Jesus let her have her way, had she
felt so exalted. And suddenly she stood on a brand new path.

We could well include the experience of Peter, who "went
out and wept bitterly" after his betrayal of Jesus (Matt. 26:57).
Why? Because Jesus had glanced at him. That one look had
been enough to change him to his inmost core. How many persons who saw Jesus had this experience!

Examples abound. Jesus was himself the therapy he practiced, as we explained in our opening pages. How it must have
shaken people, how it must have dynamized them to the depths
of their being, to have met Jesus! We read these accounts so
casually today. He spoke, he looked at him, he called, and so
on. But what actually happened? We can only surmise.

How we wish we could do the same in psychotherapy! But
this is simply out of the question. After all, we are only the

persons that we are. When something similar does happen in a session, it is only possible thanks to that incorruptible assistant of ours, the unconscious. Naturally we dare not cease to listen to its voice. But what is it like when someone recognizes his or her shadow, and then vanquishes it, as radically as may be? How does this appear in concrete practice?

A young woman who worked in a Catholic rectory suffered from a severe compulsion neurosis. She had the typical phobias: constant hand-washing, bathroom compulsion, the fear of having ingested ground glass, and so on. The whole area of marital intimacy was tabooed and beset with the gravest fears. The marriage seemed on the verge of collapse, with the young wife apparently ready for a mental hospital. But in her very first dream, she saw a female personage pointing to her and saying, with a sneer, "She's married to the parish priest!" The product of a narrow-minded, sexophobic rearing, this woman was living a factually celibate marriage. It took a strenuous, two-year analysis to bring here to the point where she could see and repel her celibate shadow. For her "graduation," to everyone's delight, she was pregnant.

A young bride, seemingly in the bloom of her youthful vitality, was escorted by her husband to analysis. Suffering from agoraphobia, she was unable so much as to leave the house unaccompanied. Whenever she had attempted to do so, she had been overwhelmed by panic, as if she were suddenly on the brink of utter and imminent catastrophe. Again a dream put us on the right track. She dreamed that she and her husband were on vacation. They sought hotel accommodations for the night. But it appeared that in every available room were three beds, and that there was always another man in one of the beds. Everywhere, then, the marriage was going to have to be *à trois*. And so in the analysis we set out in quest of this third, disturbing person in the triangle. At first the patient's agoraphobia offered a kind of alibi. After all, she was unable to take a single step without her husband, was she not? Eventually, however, the interloper was apprehended. It appeared that what would have been impossible in reality was easy enough for modern technology, and that our analysand had been spending long, blissful

evenings in the intimate company of a certain movie hero, then
all the rage. But alas, her pleasures could only be in fantasy, for
it was only on the television screen that she ever found her lover
near. It was anything but easy to make the patient accept that,
evening after evening, seated right beside her husband, she was
committing mental adultery. Her fear of the street protected
her from becoming a woman of the street. As she finally began to see this connection, the agoraphobia was dismantled and
her marriage partnership reconstructed. Strange, at times, the
intertwining paths leading to an awareness of one's shadow!

A charming man, the spoiled darling of all the women, came
to me with marriage difficulties. For him the reason was obvious. His wife was inapproachable. In particular, she had too
little interest in sex. The real problem, however, lay in his ex-
tramarital liaisons, of which his wife had never become aware
and of which he now said nothing to me. But then a powerful
dream was his rude awakening. He dreamed that, as he was
about to commence an evening of pleasure with his paramour,
a dark-clad, somewhat older, ugly, sickly looking man suddenly
entered the room, moved past the dreamer in silence, and disappeared. The man was so shocked, right in the dream, that
no further intimacies could occur in the dream. To his question
who the stranger was, I could only reply, "That's you, too. In
this dream, you saw a part of yourself that you had never seen
before. You have met your shadow." Astonishingly, the man
was so shocked by this single dream that he simply came right
out and declared, "You're right." Subsequently the couple's
marriage relations radically improved. Thanks to the shock of
that dream, with its obvious interpretation, my client had become a new person. Here again the courage for self-encounter
had led to an inward conversion.

From the last three examples, it is altogether plain that the
courage for self-encounter demanded by Jesus the therapist is, in
its essentials, our spontaneous inward acceptance of the image
of ourself in the mirror held up to us by our unconscious. In
depth psychology we call this an experience of "self-evidence."

Jesus as Victim of Shadow Projection

As long as he walked this earth, Jesus rejected any projection of
the shadow of others onto himself. Not only did he frustrate the
cries of those who attacked him with the slogan that he drove
"out devils through Beelzebub, chief of devils" (Matt.
12:24);
not only did he stand his ground against the slander leveled
against him; but he rejected positive projections, as well. He
even refused the title "Good Teacher" (Mark 10:17–18), and
he repeatedly forbade his disciples to accept similar labels. He
rejected the very title "Son of David," an allusion to his descen-
dancy from a royal house and a salutation with which he was
evidently often greeted (Matt. 22:41–46). How far he went in
thus rejecting projections upon his own person has been demonstrated by modern New Testament scholarship, which has shown
that he refused to accept the titles "Son of God," "Son of Man,"
and "Christ." Jesus was what he was, and had no need to prove
his identity by means of titles and decorations. He himself was
always more than enough.

We may forestall certain objections to these last propositions
by reminding the reader that Jesus' rejection of *titles* such as
"Son of God" and others, in no way militates against the appli-
cability to his person of the *content* of such titles of sovereignty,
which are found in the earliest tradition. We are not suggest-
ing that the *meaning* of these names did not or could not be
applied to Jesus. This is obviously a question to be determined
separately in each case.

After his departure from this world, of course, Jesus could
no longer refuse to be saddled with other people's projections,
varied and contradictory as such projections might be. After his
death words were placed in his mouth that he would never have
uttered, including at times statements diametrically contrary
to the meaning of things he actually did say. He was made
responsible for everything imaginable, and the more so as his
otherworldly exaltation became more and more explicit. No one
wished to do without him. All world religions have claimed him
in one way or another, each as its own dogmatics might prompt,
in a multi-layered process that is impossible to disregard, down

through two millennia of boisterous religious history.

With the advent of psychoanalysis, we have witnessed the development of an altogether new kind of projection over the course of the last hundred years. This type of projection is aimed specifically at the person of Jesus. By and large, it is of a disparaging, slanderous, malicious nature, and for all practical purposes constitutes a second, spiritual crucifixion.

No one has gone to further limits here than psychoanalyst Theodor Reik, one of Freud's most prominent pupils, and his friend.[5] The spearhead of Reik's approach is to set Jesus over against the enigmatic figure of Judas. Of Judas' character, of the motive of his deed, and the like, we actually know nothing. We can only make suppositions. Reik supposes the following. The rebellious strivings that agitated the subjugated, humiliated Jewish nation of those times were personified in Jesus, who permitted his enthusiasm to carry him to the commission of an out-and-out act of sedition. "These revolutionary strivings found their outlet in the rebel Jesus. The young, violent, pugnacious God of the Son succeeded to the throne of the ancient and mighty Father God dethroned by Jesus." But this occasioned an "ego split" among the Jewish people. An unbearable feeling of guilt was scarcely to be avoided — after all, Jesus had committed murder — and this overwhelming guilt had need of some way of escape, some safety valve. The latter was found in the figure of Judas. In Judas, the ancient "God of the Fathers" joined battle with Jesus' new Father God. Judas was thus the "representative of the murdered Yahweh," who in Judas' betrayal and Jesus' crucifixion now avenged himself on his murderer. We may spare ourselves the rest of the Reikian fantasies. At all events it is now Judas who is the savior, for he has rescued the God of the Fathers. Jesus is the murderer in the story. The salvific figure is Judas, not Jesus. It was Judas who offered himself as a saving sacrifice, not Jesus.

As we see, if we are looking for examples of projection, examples that will clarify its innermost substance and nature, then we can do no better than to look for them in the high priests of psychoanalysis itself. What we are confronted with here is nothing but an inextricably tangled, emotional rule by the most petty-minded, in which projection operates on an obvious chain of chimerical suppositions, and goes its blissful way, unconcerned with, and totally uninstructed by, historical actuality or objective facts. Reik's libel has been reissued by Alexander Mitscherlich, in the tragicomic, brazen hope that Reik's book will "contribute to deeper insights." A like web of projection, so emotionally and cunningly woven, is anything but science, of course. We are reminded of the woman in the example we have cited above, whose projection was so blind that the mothers-in-law were simply and sincerely interchanged, as far as the causality of the problems was concerned. The innocent one was to blame for everything. The guilty one was hailed, sheltered, and cultivated. Projections are not harmless. As we have seen, they burst forth in raging, devastating storms of emotion, and they burst forth in persons, science, and peoples. They are no more harmless than the courage to acknowledge and overcome one's shadow is pervasive.

Such courage has certainly failed those who have called themselves Jesus' disciples and witnesses down through the centuries. Here we may append some further examples to the one we have just examined. Jesus has indeed admonished us to "become as little children" — to become trusting, open, receptive, and welcoming, in all simplicity and spontaneity. But he has said nothing about wishing to be honored as a child himself. The cultus of the Babe in the manger, the Babe on Mary's lap, leads to a fine-honed theology of the child, intimately bound up with mariology itself and constituting the great humiliation and castration of Christianity, where it has made it psychologically possible to glorify, and even dogmatize, one's own infantilism and immaturity.

Jesus issues an altogether basic warning against "judging." But as we page through the New Testament itself, the further we read the more often the judge appears. We may indeed say, "The judge is at the door," for there have been times in the history of the church when Jesus has become so preeminently the judge of his faithful that Christians themselves collapsed under the image. We know of the example of Martin Luther. For Luther, as he himself recalls in the preface to his Latin works, the "door to paradise" was the realization he gained from Scripture that God "does not judge" but "bestows."

And if we include the doctrine of justification for good measure, then surely we are forced to the realization that the church dogmatics and the church itself of two millennia have actually been unable to tell us what Christ really means for us and for the world. They have generally preferred to stay with the whipping-boy theory: Christ has undergone the punishment that really should be falling on our own heads. We could ask for no finer compendium of the theory and praxis of the whipping boy.

These images of Jesus are as distasteful to enunciate as to conceptualize. One might as well take one's leave of them and practice "modern theology," where Hegel, Heidegger, Marx, and Bloch set the standard. Thus we could paint over the old, super-orthodox, de facto insupportable projections with new, somewhat less destructive ones.

We have offered the reader the merest intimation of the history of human beings who fail to rouse the courage for self-encounter. Never having become aware of their own shadow, these persons and collectivities can only continue to heap their projections, old and new, established and freshly concocted, on the image of Jesus.

Chapter 4

The Prerequisites

Analysis takes courage, and it is the therapist's task to survey the possibilities of each case and bring this courage to its maximum potential. Especially the courage for self-encounter is required, and we have seen this in detail. Here, as everywhere, the therapist's contribution is ancillary. It is the dream, rightly understood and accepted — in other words, the creative unconscious — that is the determining agent in the overall, multifaceted process of arousing this courage and engaging it to flow smoothly and at full throttle. It is the dynamics of the unconscious, liberated from within, that alone will dynamize the whole person, to the point where the client is willing to accept the informational content welling up from the unconscious, and then, in function of this information, to forge ahead in an intensive process of total change.

But what if these auxiliary, enabling efforts fail? What if the unconscious becomes, as it were, downright weary of knocking and pounding? What if nothing is heard or done? The ways of analysis are mysterious. On a soil that had seemed utterly dead, a psyche will spring into full bloom. Or a seemingly promising beginning will dwindle away to nothing. Status and rank, sophistication or simplicity, neither help nor hinder. I like to compare the hours, or sessions, of an analysis with learning to fly a glider. The analysand's psychic glider is towed aloft by a motorized aircraft piloted by the analyst. The glider remains tethered to the other aircraft for a number of hours. Eventually, however, the cadet's instruction is complete. The time comes when the glider is cut loose. This is the moment of decision. What will he do? Will she fly? Will she? To be honest, we do not know. Or at least we are not sure. At this critical point we are only excited, breathless onlookers.

The analysis has reached its hour of destiny. Now we shall see whether the client has "the right stuff." The total personality is about to come to light. What will emerge? Shall we see a personality with the wherewithal to follow through? For the therapist these are tense hours, often charged with the keenest existential empathy. The analysand frequently glides through them, grasping what has happened only in retrospect, often considerably later.

Jesus had a profound appreciation of the implications of an individual's ultimate psychic potential. Accordingly he was entirely cognizant of the unpredictability of the fertility of the soil on which the seed has fallen. Thus he creates a therapeutic paradigm of the first order: the Parable of the Seed, traditionally known as the Parable of the Sower, or, in German, as the Parable of the Different Kinds of Soil (Mark 4:1–8).

A Difference in Soils

The Parable of the Seed rings with a triple tonality. First and second come realism and certainty. Some of the seed will never grow. It will be carried off by the birds, or else it will spoil and rot. That some will be lost is an a priori certainty — sober, realistic fact. But the seed that falls on "good ground" will yield a rich, perhaps all but overwhelming, harvest. Thus the sober, realistic knowledge that human beings are of various types never degenerates into discouragement and pessimism. After all, the fertility of the soil will only become evident at harvest time.

This is how it is with the kingdom of God, Jesus says, and with its potential members, human beings, who may or may not grow to its stature. But the basic insight of the parable is more broadly valid than this. It is simply psychologically correct. The analyst, too, will be well advised to abide by an earnest realism when examining the availability of the various prerequisites —

when assessing the quality of the "soil" in various patients. At the same time, we know the unexpected, inexhaustible possibilities of the unconscious, and so our realism will always incline to the positive side.

The third attitude characterizing the Parable of the Seed consists in what we might call the acknowledgment of a quadruple polarity. There are four possible ways in which the functional terms may interrelate. The first, the prime polarity, will be that obtaining between *seed and good soil.* Ideally, seed and soil will be mutually suitable. But in the first instance in the parable, when the seed falls on the hard path, or in the second, when it falls on stony ground, or in the third, when it is strangled by briers — the prime, correct, effective polarity is disturbed. Hence the possibility of three secondary, undesirable polarities: in terms of the parable, *seed and hard path, seed and stony soil,* and *seed and thorns.* Only in the fourth case set forth in the parable does the genuine, the true, the good and normal, polarity materialize: that obtaining between the seed and good soil. But even here there are various manners in which this materialization may occur.

The first two attitudes of the parable — realism and certitude — show us beyond any doubt that Jesus sees people to be different. We are fairly awash in the difference and the variety that distinguish the human beings around us in every imaginable respect. Jesus is no equalizer. If any parable says it, this one does: *this* is the way people are. People are different, and there is no getting around it. Jesus' attitude gainsays any ideological levelling in this respect. Jesus acknowledges diversity, in every regard that may concern us. He always accepts that diversity as a given. When all human beings come to be regarded as the same, an abstract image of the human being enters the picture, supplanting the concrete one, and invariably appearing in function of some ideological need or other to place certain human beings under a ban. And suddenly what Jesus is saying becomes completely unintelligible. The richest element of the parable for depth psychology is its third attitude: the recognition of a variety of polarities, an authentic one, and a number of disturbed or disordered ones. Here, from the viewpoint of depth psychology, the parable becomes a paradigm par excellence for any anthropology, theological, philosophical, or psychological. Are the signs of the times calling out to us to understand and grasp Jesus' meaning?

Receptivity Extinguished

First, then, we have the beaten path — the hard, much trodden way. This comparison obviously visualizes individuals so hardened, and thereby narrowed, in their awareness that when confronted with an invitation to creativity — when approached and collared by a challenge — the only response of which they are capable is not to let it get anywhere near them. Any attempt arising within them to render them less rigid, to give them a new orientation, to endow them with a broadening creativity, shrivels and dies. Theirs is the beaten path, and always will be. They are persons of extinguished receptivity. The fire of creative acceptance has sputtered out. This happens. And Jesus, being a realist, says it happens. Later, in the times of the church, a doctrine of the "restoration of all" will develop, and the meaning of the Parable of the Seed will disappear from view. Other New Testament loci, regarded by solid scholarship today as being of a secondary value, will be appealed to in its place. There *are* individuals whose inner being is like a rock-hard beaten path, Jesus says. He is simply observing a fact.

Seed that falls on the beaten path will not be long in falling prey to the birds. Indeed, it will actually attract them. It is just the same with human beings. Rock-hard interiority — quenched receptivity — actually attracts the "birds" of our parable, and they will pluck up the seed and carry it off. And a human being's last hope will be gone.

What are these birds? The symbol of the bird is a clear reference to a particular mental or spiritual moment. It represents the spirit that soars, that flies where it will — everywhere over the earth, at any rate, higher and higher under heaven. Thus the Holy Spirit is symbolized by a dove. In mythology, in the folk tale, in saga, in the dream, birds appear as helpful companions, counselling, warning, guiding. A bird peering in a window is a sign of good luck. But like any other symbol, the bird is ambivalent. It can be positive or negative. And only the context will determine which of the two it is to be. In the Parable of the Seed the birds obviously play a negative role. They rob and plunder what was destined for growth. "Birds croak calamity," we say. On account of birds Hansel and Gretel would now perish utterly, since it was the birds of the air who plucked away the bread crumbs that Hansel had managed to drop to mark the children's way home again. Now the children are lost in the wood forever. A hero lies chained to a rock while an eagle plucks his liver from his breast. I have a tapestry of the High Stations, or deeds, of Saint Martin, embroidered in twelve medallions. One medallion depicts the saint in his preaching role, while all about him birds enact the burden of his sermon. They plunge headlong to the earth, and unless their intended victims, human beings, exercise constant vigilance, these incarnations of evil will snatch them up in their sharp beaks and whisk them off in an instant, before they so much as perceive their catastrophe. The birds in our parable are only acting according to their nature, but here as well the context in which they appear shows them as symbols of the destructive.

The destructive birds, and the beaten path, are set in mutual correspondence or polarity. Only where many have walked can the seed lie so open to view that it actually attracts the birds. The poles condition and reinforce each other. There are no coincidences — least of all in depth psychology. The path symbolizes the hard-packed, unreceptive psyche. And the birds of devastation? They too, in this mighty metaphor, are *destructive functionalities of that same psyche.*

The challenge of the creative has encountered a quenched receptivity. The latter, instead of becoming more open, will now become even more rigidly, more ironly, more fanatically destructive than before, in the case represented by this part of our parable. A psyche that has turned destructive will actually provoke the psychic functionalities and reactions to pluck up any crumb of creative dynamics that may have been sown, any seed of positive development that may have been broadcast, and annihilate it. In other words it is the psyche itself that, like a powerful solenoid, will switch over or redirect any positive current appearing within it to the circuit marked "Destruct." It would be a grossly erroneous interpretation of the motif of the birds in our parable, and betoken a total neglect of the facts of depth psychology, were we to wish to see the birds simply as symbols of some external destiny, something fated and doomed, some unlucky coincidence. The causality of a psyche's quenched receptivity lies with that same psyche. Thus the annihilation of any future creative contact is the individual psyche's own doing.

No excuses are to be read into the parable, as some environmental theory or behaviorist psychology might be tempted to do. The task of depth psychology is ever the *unemotional discovery of the facts*. An analytical assessment reveals this particular psyche to be structured in *this particular way* at the moment. This individual, concrete psyche presently hosts a dynamic action of this particular kind. Now it will be possible to appraise the possibilities, the potential, of this concrete psyche. Depth psychology's principal task is not to observe material that basks in the light of consciousness, but to ferret out the psyche's hidden impulses and operations. Freud and Jung were both right, then, in their stubborn insistence that analysis is science — *pace* the recent critics who would like to regard this position precisely as their principal error.[1] No, there is no speculation or explanation here, and no excuses. It is not a question of who is right and who is wrong; it is a question of the facts. These facts are to be objectively established and demonstrated, as a skilled surgeon, with a few practiced strokes of the scalpel, can lay open an inflamed appendix. Once we have a clear picture of the objective state of things, the means of correcting it emerge practically of themselves. Any theorizing, any philosophizing, any metaphysicizing, would only corrupt the procedure. Depth psychology, from beginning to end, must be *distanced objectivity*.

How do these psychological "birds" of ours actually present themselves? First and foremost come the ideologies, the sectarianisms, and so forth — and of course that kind of "conservatism" that, since the days of Adam, has always "known better." In the presence of a like mentality, constructive new possibilities, creative new departures, dare not even signal their presence. We have an interesting example in the case of Sigmund Freud himself. Anyone styling religion a priori as "neurosis" will of course deal with any religious phenomenon after the manner of the birds in the Parable of the Seed. An ossified legalism of Jesus' time likewise manifested itself as the hard, beaten path of spiritual unreceptivity, where the psychic functionalities imitate the birds of Jesus' parable and pounce on the seed of creativity. Jesus speaks often, and only too correctly, of the possibility of a hardening of the heart precisely vis-à-vis the overtures of the creative.

Jesus' approach is objective, then, and herein he is our model par excellence. He attempts no explanations, he offers no reasons. Least of all does he excuse. Laconically, pithily, *he observes*. There *are* such individuals — persons like paths that have been packed down until they are as hard as stone, persons without a spark of receptivity left in their souls.

That there are such individuals, Jesus experienced only too concretely in matters concerning his own person. He was in league with all the evil spirits, he was told. "This one slanders God," was the cry in his ear (Matt. 9:3). And down swooped the birds. It was the only way. Too many persons in Jesus' collectivity had this sort of "hardened heart," and Jesus was plucked away.

Persons whose receptivity has been utterly quenched are seldom seen in analysis. The mere fact that they come for therapy permits us to suppose that there will be some receptivity here, at least minimal or vestigial. At all events as psychotherapists we have not the least objective right to make a judgment like: "Everything really looks dead there, inside you!" We are not clairvoyants. We have not the slightest grounds, however discouraging the prognosis, for a claim to be able to foretell the actual highways and byways of the unconscious. The latter will have its way, in utter disregard of our solemn pronouncements. We do, however, see *extreme cases,* and by no means infrequently. There are instances in which, at the time of treatment, not even a minimum of openness will be in evidence. And yet experience teaches that even here there may be a delayed effect, after months or even years. Let us examine a few of these extreme cases. They will by no means be identical with the cases of resistance that we have discussed above. The instances we are about to cite have an unhappy ending of their own. The problem may lie in a crippling lack of the emotional capacity to communicate, or a lethal intellectualism, or a numb, monotonous psyche, or any other extremely "hardened" condition.

I had a teacher in therapy who had been born and bred in what is now East Germany but who at the end of World War II was released in the West. His prominent Nazi past prevented him from securing a professional foothold in the West, so he decided to try his luck in the East, in the German Democratic Republic (DDR). Here he managed to secure an appointment, albeit at the price of any ideals or scruples, as a teacher of working-class people in the widest variety of establishments and enterprises. His was the task of propagandizing the DDR ideology with the workers and stirring them up against the owners. But the prosperity of the Golden West proved too much of an attraction, and he switched loyalties. Behold, he was now a well-heeled citizen of the Federal Republic. Psychosomatic symptoms drove him to therapy, but his double brainwashing, which he had brought on himself, had generated in him the iron-bound conviction that he had done the right thing in every situation. Then what actual need had he of therapy? And his treatment was as ineffectual as was his velleity to be helped.

A lawyer came for therapy, fraught with the impenetrable persona she had constructed. By "persona" we mean the outer form or appearance of our personhood that we hold forth to our environment in function of our social position. Now, here was a lawyer to the core. Wrapped in the lawyer persona as if it had been a suit of armor, professionally steeped in an atmosphere of judgment-passing and court cases, not even in analysis did she withdraw one whit from her ingrained habits of thinking. With dictatorial, coldly logical judgments she rejected any attempt to offer an interpretation of a dream. She held to her neurosis as steadfastly and consistently as she took a case to court.

A member of the Jehovah's Witnesses seemed entirely willing to respond to the demands of an analytical treatment. It was clear to her that there could be no reservations — that openness, spontaneity, and veracity would be the basic conditions for going ahead. I was somewhat puzzled by her attitude, as one is only too familiar with the stubbornness of the Witnesses in their so-called faith convictions, and their soaring pretensions to infallibility. And so I emphasized this point once more. It must be perfectly clear, I told her, that when the manifestations of the unconscious called for it, even the faith convictions she held as a Jehovah's Witness would have to be submitted to the analytic process. That was clear, she replied — and then she added, downright triumphantly: "No problem! Our faith is scientifically proved!" I asked the young woman how long she had been studying the Bible. "Two years," came the assured answer. "Well," I said, "I've been at it for forty years, and I'm not always so sure of myself." My client gaped at me in complete astonishment. She never came back. Members of sects often turn out to be impossible to help. The towering claims of their ideology, with its demand for total submission, tend to quench their personal receptivity in a very particular way.

A colleague from Israel gave a shattering report at a conference. He had had the experience of attempting to treat adult Jews who as children had had to live in German concentration camps. With many of them, he reported, analytic treatment was simply impossible. Cruelty and terror had not only crippled or impaired their psychic powers, it had destroyed them. There is such a thing as "psychic wipeout" — emotional devastation that leaves no possibilities for psychic growth whatever. Only maintenance therapy enables these individuals to continue to exist at all. Here, however, we are dealing with existential experiences of an extreme order, which reduce to silence any appraisal in terms of depth psychology and render any therapy utterly impossible.

Basically, however, and by way of a summary of the foregoing, we may say: No ideology, no brainwashing at the hands of a system, no intellectualism, no self-absolutizing doctrine, no positivism, no Cartesianism that would see the human being as part of a great cosmic machine, no behaviorism with its explanation

of everything in terms of manipulability — in brief, no "ism" and
no false teaching — can in and of itself make of a person a beaten
path, simply automatically, however exposed to their influence
that person may be. Everything depends on the psychic prerequisites, which furnish the celebrated psychic "coathangers"
for this element or that, and then determine whether gradually more destructive psychic reactions are to take flight like
vultures — or not.

Flash in the Pan

"Some seed fell on stony ground, where there was but little soil.
It sprouted at once, as the thin topsoil was soaked with dew.
But no sooner did the sun come out than the sprouts dried up
and died. The roots had not been able to pierce the ground"
(Mark 4:5–6). Where this second type of soil is concerned, we
might say in the spirit of aphorism: "The sun will bring all
things to light."

The underlying rock is too near the surface. Thus the whole
seedling, when it sprouts, is confined to the surface, and on the
surface it will wither when the sun burns hot overhead. What
happens in this second type of person is in a way even more
disappointing than what occurs with the first. The first type of
person Jesus sketches promises nothing. The second promises a
great deal, and delivers nothing. Here the disturbed polarity is
that of sun and stony ground. The parable is of course a product
of the Eastern perception. In the lands of the Middle East the
sun not only shines; it glows like a red-hot iron, withering all
that it touches. Even the symbol of the sun is ambivalent, then.
The sun is the source of all life force. And yet in mythology
it can appear on the scene like a rampaging lion. In the case
before us, too, its function is negative. It brings to light the
deep neuroticism of the personalities concerned. And so once
again the quality of the soil has not been designated at random.
There is a very definite rationale why it is "stony" this time.

"Stony soil" analysands, to speak in the language of the
parable, make a splendid beginning. But they are *wetterwend-
isch*, as Luther translates — they change with the weather. They

fairly waft into the office, borne on a cloud of enthusiasm and joyous anticipation. They hang on the analyst's lips. They are prepared to understand and grasp everything. Their favorite word is, "Naturally!" They are amiable and are preponderantly of the type that likes to bring flowers and gifts. They are so excited — the turning point of their life is in sight. And suddenly they are gone!

We are dealing with a reaction of a psyche that is actually capable of no real commitment. It wriggles away from the mildest test or trial. This is the danger especially with patients whose strong faculty is intuition, and who are without a balancing critical function to broaden their reference to reality.

I had a master toolmaker in therapy, whose personal life, owing to an intense mother-attachment, was one of isolation and complete lack of motivation. He would spend his weekends simply sitting in his room staring into space and brooding. A strong, tall young man, he sat completely helpless before me. But he was glad that he had finally made a contact, as he repeatedly assured me. Then he reported the following dream, among others. "The master himself was here," he began. That is, Carl Jung was speaking with me in my office. From the outset, then, this dream announced that its meaning would be very special. It would appeal to the highest authorities. The analysand himself, the dream went on, waited in the corridor, but eavesdropped at the door, as a young child might. Then he dreamed he heard Jung give his considered opinion concerning his other dreams: "Well and good. But, you see, all that is in question now. The young man is too sensitive." During our difficult discussion of this dream my client and I agreed that he might well go on a little outing the following Sunday, to the vicinity of Speyer, to see the cathedral and the graves of the Emperors.

My client's analysis terminated as suddenly and unexpectedly as its brief commencement had been hopeful. He never returned. He regressed into the defiant stage of a three-year-old child, and my only contact with him thereafter was the receipt of a snappish letter, without salutation or signature, in which he let me have it, again the way a young child might. The opening analytic steps had seemed to presage a successful outcome. But they were totally annihilated by the first, really quite harmless, challenges of that analysis. In the language of the parable, whatever promise the commencement might have held, it burned up very quickly in the heat of trial.

Another client of this type, a pilot, came to therapy not only willingly, but in a blaze of enthusiasm, and of course he felt that sentiment to be entirely spontaneous and genuine. "I'm so glad to be here!" he said. "It's like being on a date!" On one occasion he came back from Nice with fifty carnations for me. He actually enjoyed his own contrition: "I came in like a roaring lion," he explained at the end of one of our sessions, "but I'm going to leave as meek as a lamb." And yet the roots could not pierce the soil, to use the language of our biblical text.

I especially remember an office clerk I had in treatment, a woman who suffered from a massive mother-attachment. At work, she spoke her mind and made decisions. But the moment she returned home, she was her mother's little girl again — indecisive, without initiative, depressive, and so on. Enthusiastically she learned that analysis opens the way to freedom and independence. She completely understood that her own dreams were to guide the way. Her first steps toward independence were energetic ones — for example, she moved out of her mother's house and began living alone. Session after session, her insights were remarkable. "I was so glad..." was her characteristic expression. Then suddenly it was all over. Her new home was often empty now, as the little girl crept back under her mother's wing for comfort and consolation. Moreover, her depressions grew even worse. And all of this occurred without obvious grounds — apart from the main grounds, which were that her euphoria had simply run out of steam. Her inner potential had revealed itself as inadequate. "The sun came out" — and there were her habits, her upbringing, her whole formation, patiently waiting for her.

Why did the toolmaker back out so quickly, almost as soon as he had begun? Why did the pilot promise so much and then deliver nothing? Why did the office clerk start out so energetically and then so very suddenly drop out of the race? Here we touch on the mystery enunciated in our parable — the mystery of the person, of its essential core, of its "self," as the wisdom of the East would have it. Entelechies can be great or small, Aristotle would say. There are shining "ideas," Plato would tell us, and there are those that only glow in the dark. There are strong monads, Leibniz would tell us, that grow by leaps and bounds as they move from engagement to engagement, and there are little monads that shatter to smithereens under pressure of the slightest demand. There are different soils, Jesus says, and so there are different harvests. Can and can't, will and won't, the intensity that fairly explodes and the frail little push that gradually shrivels up and withers, constitute the inner mystery of persons and their concrete human lives. And we could lengthen our list of some of the more modern attempts to elucidate this mystery. But every attempt makes the same finding: the quality of the soil is a mystery of existence. And this last proposition is the quintessence of all the deeper anthropologies of all times.

Strangling Collectivity

Jesus has no illusions. Much is lost, this he knows. No good comes of the third type of person he portrays, either. "Some seed fell on thorny ground, and was soon overgrown and smothered by thorny weeds" (Mark 4:7).

At harvest time both the weeds and the ripe grain are cut down. The weeds are burned, the grain is brought into the barn. However, when planting time comes again, the deeper roots of the weeds are still in the ground. So the weeds grow far more rapidly than the new sprouts, and soon they have strangled the new shoots just as they had the season before. Of course, there is not just one clump of weeds in a field; many thistles and thorns have very long runners, so that they cover the field with a veritable carpet of roots, and weeds shoot up everywhere. The birds, in our first case, came by ones, twos, or groups; but the weeds surprise us everywhere. One often sees such fields in the East, lying fallow, abandoned to weeds of every type.

The image chosen here is a fine metaphor of the mass mentality — of the collectivity, as we say in psychology. Thus the

psychological translation of Jesus' third type of person will be:
A great deal of seed is strangled by the collectivity. Jesus' third
picture, then, is as skillfully constructed and as pithy as the first
two. Here the disturbed polarity is: seed and thorns.

Jesus is obviously thinking of the collectivity of his own day,
with which he came into daily confrontation.[2] Of course he has
already created the great symbol of the collectivity — the im-
mortal figure of the formally honorable, inwardly corrupt Pharisee, since become a universal cultural and religious symbol in
East and West alike. "Collectivity," as we use it here, is a technical term. It does not simply designate a people or community.
A people or community can always degenerate into a collectivity, however, and does so whenever it obstructs the authentic
development of the individual personality, especially when it
strangles that personality by police methods, as for instance in
socialist states today, or indeed in any of the dictatorships or
police states of all times. In such polities only *one* standard
of thought and behavior exists, the official one, and any devi-
ation is severely dealt with. That is a collectivity. In Jesus'
collectivity, every area of life, public and private, was all but
mechanically regulated by the "Law." The law of God, traditionally regarded as good, had degenerated into a murderous
legalism that killed spirit and life.

The psychological counterpart of the collectivity is the "in-
trojection" or interiorization of this legalism. The latter becomes so intimate and personal to our own thought and conscience that we are ready to swear that it is our own hallowed
conviction. Now we fall victim to the general norm. We are
careful not to poke our head above our assigned rung on the
collective ladder. We have fallen victim to the collective frustration. Now we are not only conscious; we are conscious with
the same inner conviction as is everyone else. In our relation to
reality as to ourselves, we are now nothing more than a "someone." As Jung put it, the outer collective has become the "inner
collective."

In the parable of the seed, Jesus represents the collectivity
(external or internal, it makes no difference for the moment)
as stifling, strangling weeds. He surely strove to uproot this

noxious growth wherever he might. He roundly branded the prevailing piety of the Torah as hypocrisy. He rightly characterized the anxious observance of ritual purity as a cowardly flight from the only cleanliness that matters: interior purity. He pilloried the insensitivity and brutality of society toward the weak, especially toward women. His daring diatribes excoriated the representatives of law and piety as thieves, liars, and, once more, sanctimonious hypocrites. He took sharp exception to the spirit of social caste that created untouchables of, especially, tax collectors and Samaritans. This of course is only a sketchy sampling of the list of battles waged by Jesus in the major engagement to which he was led by his wholesale commitment to the uprooting of the weeds of the external, and especially of the internal, legalistic collectivity.

The part of our parable dealing with the thorny ground reflects a total, comprehensive picture of a culture and a religion. And it signals a battle to the death, in the most desperate, most comprehensive action that has ever been waged against a culture and a religion.

The metaphor of the thorny ground is still very apt. We are simply surrounded by thistles and nettles today, and not only in the polities of coercion and repression to which we have referred, but in the modern collectivity across the board. Its victims sit in our offices. Should we wish to consider this collectivity more closely, we should gain some further insight merely by reflecting that nearly every patient coming to us for therapy suffers primarily or secondarily from depression. Today, depression leads to suicide (or, more frequently, to suicide attempts). When a prospective client appears on our doorstep without any symptoms of depression, we know that we shall be dealing with a very exceptional case. What are these weeds shooting up everywhere around us? Their genotype is precisely the one characterized by Jesus. Their phenotype will of course have its own specificity.

The autonomous collectivity-complexes of our day operate primarily by way of their *constant robbery of our existence and security.* Today's human being is forced into a preestablished pattern by the *state,* which swears it is a democracy but which has long since become the authoritarian dictatorship of a party.

Party discipline has replaced personal conscience. Let the latter dare to stir, and the disloyal maverick who owns it will promptly be brought to reason by force. In other countries of the Western world, appeals to the highest court of the land in an alarmingly increasing number of cases demonstrate the failure of all other protest of the rape of truth and the assault on right.

Today's human beings are diminished in their humanity by the wholesale degeneration of the surrounding culture. Cheap talk, calling the self-evident into question, is "in." Since nothing is certain any longer, no one must ever dare to look like an expert. Rather — and our philosophers and theologians bravely second the motion — let the mighty word of Götz von Berlichingen prevail ("Kiss my — !"). Yes, Götz von Berlichingen would be flabbergasted to learn that he has become the ancestor of a new treatment: scream therapy, in which obscene four-letter words are belted out for hours at a time if need be. This is intended to relieve pressure. Actually it is the perfect way to get in training and stay in shape. The Japanese knew that in World War II. They kept their recruits screaming for hours on end, as they lunged at dummies of the American enemy. And surely enough, when it was for keeps, these same fine young men just lunged away without another thought.

Today's human beings are strangled in their differentiation, in the variety of their *humanum,* through the general decomposition or *degradation of ethos.* This is not Great-Grandfather's lament that things ain't the way they used to be. No, the new decline is genuine, precisely because everybody goes along. Abortion? Yawn. Sex deluge? So what else is new. Our own sex life has lost its intimacy anyway, and the banalization of sex no longer seems the degradation of anything special. Who keeps a promise today? What or whom can you trust? The order of the day is tolerance: whatever else you do, cause no pain. In other words maintain a crippled sense of values.

Today's human being comes under indictment for the pollution of the *environment.* What canned goods contain no harmful preservatives? Which nuclear plant is the last to have had another leak? Air and water contamination, ecological devastation on all sides, have sent the human being into exile. Now we are

homeless in the deepest sense. Indeed, our sheer numbers over-
whelm us: how can you "make yourself at home" when your feet
are constantly being stepped on?

Human beings today are the victims of a depredation of
their existence precisely by reason of their own unbridled *con-*
sumerism. A Mercedes used to be a status symbol. Now every sales rep has one. What Jones has, Smith simply must
acquire. We build our dream-houses — not that we can begin
to pay for them — and thereby thrust the achievement neurosis even deeper down inside. We slave for pennies because we
need a hundred thousand dollars. This ubiquitous, senseless
consumerism, this indiscriminate craving of ours transforms the
whole of our lives into one senseless, convulsive achievement fixation, which sucks any authentic *joie de vivre* into its maelstrom
of self-flagellation. And our lives are obliterated.

Our utterly uninhibited consumerism transforms each and
every item that falls within our perception into an *exploitable*
object, including, and especially, nature and its living creatures.
There is a forest near Heidelberg in which trees display informational shields informing the vacationer of the ideal industrial
utility of each. There used to be a woods here. Now there is
just wood. Or take the recently completed concentration camp
for lambs in the vicinity of Stuttgart. To be sure, the torture is
elegantly styled "intensive animal husbandry," and the papers
ran a story about the fresh lamb that will now be on the mar-
ket three times a year: "Meat Supply Gap Closed." Here we
raise no more livestock. We produce meat. These are but two
examples. The actual list is endless. That a beast in human
custody has a title to humane care, that human beings have an
obligation to treat animals in a humane way if for no other reason than for the sake of the human beings — all this is forgotten
now, drowned in a flood of consumer craving. We have forgotten that once upon a time a certain Albert Schweitzer called
"reverence for life" the only true, humane, and universal ethic.
Such obliviousness to reality only points up our ever more serious poisoning of our collective mentality through our brutal,
thoughtless insensitivity. This anesthesia, this throttling of the
feelings, so that I no longer ask what a thing is worth in itself

but only wonder what good it might be to me, indicates nothing short of a comprehensive regression to subhuman behavior levels. Surely the increasing frequency of cannibal dreams today should astonish no one.

This is but one of the many collective compulsions and psychic burdens that lie at the root of the growing frequency of depressive illnesses, hitherto unknown in their present dimensions.

Depression is essentially neuroticized grief. Thus we may logically ask: over what? Why do these masses of human beings grieve? They grieve over the rapidly receding possibility of living their human lives in a human way. They grieve from a sense that, as members of ever larger groups, they have long since become objects of exploitation themselves, right along with the trees and the lambs. Their confinement of any concern for their environment to the area of utility alone — the only concern of which consumerism and craving have left them capable — has long since emerged as a trenchant indictment of their own lives.

In terms of the image presented by our parable, we are gradually being throttled. Jesus suggests no route of escape for this comprehensive type. Is there one for us today?

Let us consider a few actual cases. An unemployed waitress was completely incapacitated for work by her very severe depressions. Among her dreams, she dreamt she had concocted her own breasts into a dish to be served to her male guests. But the latter only picked at them, without appetite or interest. Here the symbol of the feminine, served in such abundance to so many, becomes a symbol of today's cheap sex. In her youth my client had practiced just such cheap sex, failing to notice the loss of humanness she was incurring by serving herself up in this manner. Only her later depressions brought this to light. The whole dream is a veritable model protest of the transformation of femaleness into a consumer item.

Of course there is the male counterpart. A member of the board of directors of a certain corporation came for therapy complaining of depression and insomnia. In one of his dreams, he goes on a business trip. As usual, he takes a room in the most elegant hotel of the city. The manager personally escorts him to his suite, courteously showing him its fine appointments. In the bathroom, to his astonishment, the dreamer sees lying in the bathtub a naked woman, who gives him a come-hither look. She is simply one of the conveniences of a luxury suite! Not that he found the woman especially attractive, but he dreamt he got into the tub with her anyway. Here is a drastic criticism of the collective slogan of our consumer society: Get what you can while you can.

A woman who likewise came in for her depression had led a life that can only be described as uninhibited. She reported the following dream. She was setting the table in her dining room. But instead of staying horizontal, the table top would tilt into an inclined plane. Despite the dreamer's repeated attempts to place three child's drinking cups on the table, they always rolled off. In the course of our discussion of this dream, it emerged that my client knew and used the expression, "down the chute." Intuitively I asked how many abortions she had had. The woman was shocked. At the same time she felt a certain liberation. As we discussed these three admitted abortions, my client recounted a nightmare she had had immediately thereafter. She had dreamt she saw three tiny coffins, and heard a voice: "Are they your children?" "Yes, Lord," she had replied, and started awake in a cold sweat. The experience failed to deter her from sacrificing four more pregnancies to the sexual collectivity, however. Here was someone really strangled by thorns. And surely enough, all attempts at analysis proved fruitless.

It is precisely cheap, casual abortions that drive women to our offices with depressions at about the time they would have given birth. Once upon a time they stood at the barricades, shock troops in the battle for the "right to our own bodies." Now they sit before us, little, pitiable messes. Their psyche has been unable to surmount the barbarity of their abortions. Our legislators know nothing of this, of course, and the so-called experts they consult, still less.

The wife of a middle management employee "just couldn't hack it" any longer, and an otherwise routine daily discussion got out of hand. Sure they'd built a new house. So had everybody else. The challenge of today's collectivity is not merely to keep up with the Joneses, but to get ahead of them! And soon the couple was crushed beneath a mountain of debts. To have a second income the wife went to work in a pencil factory, where, under pressure of exhausting, mind-numbing assembly-line work for a pittance, she succumbed to depressions and suffered a breakdown. The actual cause? The collectivity, with its overexacting claims, its unbearable, utterly excessive demands. We cite this case because it is typical of so many. I once heard a colleague call such collapses "psychic home-construction ruins."

The psychological type Jesus sketches here is far more current, and far more threatening, than we may surmise. We all live in this collective brier bush. It strangles everything it touches, and we are insufficiently aware of its threat to our existence. Jesus knew that this mode of living can only end in catastrophe. Many insightful persons among us guess it, and psychotherapy can establish it, but the catastrophe seems inevitable.

Receptivity

But "some of the seed fell on good ground, where it sprouted and grew. And some yielded thirtyfold, some sixtyfold, and some a hundredfold" (Mark 4:9). Here at last, instead of a disturbed polarity, the normal polarity prevails: seed and good soil. Thus as we come to the good soil, the three negative cases of our parable are followed by three positive ones.

"Some of the seed fell on good ground...." What is good ground? First of all it will not be hard and packed down, like the first kind of soil. It will be good, loose topsoil. Second, however, it will not be merely a thin layer of topsoil; it will be deep earth, fertilized and "worked," or turned over. Finally, it will not be overgrown with thistles and nettles; it will be what a farmer proudly calls "good soil" — where seed can sprout and seedlings thrive. What does all of this mean in psychological terms — loose, deep soil, without suffocating weeds? It means readiness to receive, receptivity.

No integration, no individuation, no healing, no spiritual development, no conversion, no renewal, no rebirth — nothing whatever in the area of psychic growth — is possible without receptivity. Receptivity — or in any case a will to the same, however diminutive, however tentative — makes sick persons well, gets derailed psyches back on track, makes the dull wise. Receptivity is everything! One must be able to receive, or learn to do so, or else the empty pot remains just that.

In the hope of gaining some little insight into the *absolutely basic, key functionality of receptivity,* let us examine some examples of receptivity at work. An internationally known violinist of my acquaintance, recently deceased, was standing one evening at her fireplace, stirring her soup, when suddenly she seemed to hear music playing in her mind. "Now the thing was not to miss a note," she told me afterwards. When the music stopped she hurried to her writing desk. "Getting it down is always a lot harder," she remarked. But at last her latest composition was complete. "I'm absolutely helpless. I only know how to listen," she used to say.

How many examples of such power of expression could we find in the great art of all the centuries! I know personally of an equally striking instance in the world of sculpture, recounted to me on a visit by the Bolivian sculptor Marina Núñez del Prado. On the occasion of an exhibition of her work in New York, a certain gentleman, impressed with what he had seen, approached her with the request that she create a bust of his wife. But as it appeared that the man's wife had died, and that no photograph of her was to be had, the sculptor felt obliged to decline. Such a commission would surely be impossible to execute, Marina explained to the gentleman. The latter, however, was certain that she would be able to carry it off. Marina agreed to try the unusual experiment. She met her client at her studio, where she asked him not to describe his wife externally, but simply to talk about her as a person, recounting their long life together as his heart would move him to speak. Marina began to work her lump of clay. As she proceeded, to her astonishment the features of an individual whom she had never seen began to materialize under her fingers. The moment came when the gentleman asked her to stop her work. "There she is! That's my wife!" he cried, and insisted that Marina do nothing further. Any change now could only weaken the impression, he told her. What had Marina done? She had acceptingly, receptively, listened — nothing more — and formed in the clay what she had heard with her ears and mind. I must say that this is the most extraordinary instance of artistic receptivity that I have ever encountered.

The spirit of acceptance, of conscious openness, *the spirit of creative receptivity actually knows no bounds.* Jesus is absolutely correct: "Even if your trust is only as big as a mustard seed, you can tell a mountain, 'Get over there,' and it will do it. Then you'll be able to do *anything*" (Matt. 17:20). The trust of which Jesus is speaking must of course not be restricted to the so-called religious area. It is not identical with theology and dogmatics. It refuses to allow itself to be walled into any ecclesial or sectarian space. No one has a lease on it, no one can lay exclusive claim to it. It consists of a *primordial capacity for creative existence,* a potential that would have its way in the most difficult, indeed in all, domains of life and action. It is a drive that would like to seize upon the total human being, together with that human being's whole environment, in as universal fashion as possible. It is a thrust toward the human being's total coupling to that all-enabling, primordial ground of all creative being that we ultimately call God, who is symbolized in Jesus' parable as the sower.

Without receptivity there can be no very great *humanum.* Sri Aurobindo, the greatest yogi and philosopher of modern India, expresses this in the following words:

> In littleness of being lies no happiness. But the I is by its nature littleness of being. With the I the shrinking of consciousness commences, and the shrinking of consciousness inaugurates the limitation of true insight — a profound incapacitating ignorance, an imprisonment and reduction of one's life power, the rejection of kindliness, love, and understanding, the shattering of the joy of being, pain and suffering.[3]

Thus we must break out of the little world of the I. We do so when we open ourselves in receptivity to a world of higher values, and genuine being.

How does this "new becoming," which Jesus represents in

his parable as a bountiful harvest, express itself in actual therapy? Let us begin with the case of a young woman who as a child had been the victim of acts of criminal incest in the form of sexual abuse by her father. She was now beset with profound developmental disturbances of every sort, physical and psychic. Several times a year she had to be hospitalized for the most varied manifestations of her condition. And of course there was no question of her having a satisfying sexual relationship. She decided to undergo psychotherapeutic treatment. The treatment was difficult, as might be expected. But it opened up an altogether unexpected and effective potential within her. As her positive development reached a climax, she had this dream: She saw an ear of wheat, swelling with rich, ripe grain, wash up out of the ocean. Here the image of the fertile ground is replaced by that of the sea, which represents the deepest, most creative stratum of the human psyche. This stratum, this soil, had actually borne fruit. Not only has this young woman never had to return to the hospital, but she has actually been able to assume a position of leadership in her profession. She bears many permanent scars on her soul. But she is able to lead an active, liberated life.

I once had an exhibitionist in therapy. Here was a sexual perversion regarded in current academic theory as all but impossible to treat. I explained to him quite honestly that this could be no more than an experiment, as the outcome was anything but certain. I thought it would be worthwhile simply to see what the unconscious would have to offer in such a case by way of a positive potential for health, if indeed it had anything to offer at all. In terms of our approach in this chapter, I hoped to see what inner prerequisites for healing might be at hand. Anything having to do with his perversion, however, was remarkably absent from any of his dream material. By contrast, there was a great deal about his personality stagnation practically across the board, at all levels of human relationship and communication. But the man was ready and willing to respond to whatever suggestions his unconscious might make in the direction of new ways of relating or demands for a belated maturation. Suddenly we were in the presence of genuine development, and eventually all manifestations of the man's sexual deviancy disappeared.

Of course, a delicate question remained. When might he be released on his own responsibility? The answer was given in a dream. The patient dreamed that he went into a bakery shop to buy a sugar tart as a gift for his analyst. It had to be perfectly intact, he explained to the salesperson, and he rejected a tart shown him because its crust had begun to crumble a bit. Only one tart in the shop suited his requirements. But it had been sold, he learned to his chagrin. Insistently, he indicated his urgent, immediate need for this particular tart, and the salesperson acceded to his importunities. My client listened in astonishment to my explanation of his dream. It announced the termination of his therapy. The round tart was a symbol of totality. It had to be flawless: nothing might be left unfinished. It must be delivered today: the psyche itself recognizes and determines the proper moment for the termination of analysis. Finally, it was a gift for his analyst, to say farewell: in our countries a patient customarily presents the analyst with a token of appreciation at the close of the analysis, a symbol of the common endeavor that has knit them together during these long months, as well as of the "harvest" that now is the fruit of their toil.

Let us look at one last example of the harvest to be reaped in therapy when the analytic seed falls on good soil. A young husband underwent analysis for his general insecurity, timidity, lack of initiative, extremely negative self-image, and grave anxiety in his professional work. It emerged almost at once that he was suffering from a serious parental fixation, and that this was the reason why he had been unable to build an independent life. Only when he dreamed that his mother wanted to slaughter him was he shocked out of his childish dependency on his parents. Now he was willing to pay the price of becoming an independent and responsible husband and father. He even became willing to change professions, taking up a line of work better suited to his personality. Here once more, the termination of the therapy was announced by a dream. He dreamt he had come for his final session. He looked for a place to sit, but to his surprise all of the cushions in the chairs had been removed. The one chair without upholstering turned out to be too small. As he continued to search for a place to sit, the analyst entered the room, pointed to the table, and said, "Oh, just sit there." And she indicated a table with a riding saddle on it. "By the way," the analyst added, "I'm going to be away for quite a while." The patient understood this dream himself, and reported it laughing. No more easy chairs in analysis for him! His unconscious, in the guise of the analyst, now demanded he get into the saddle and ride forth to life's struggle alone. Analysis had completed its task and taken its leave. The seed had grown and ripened. The time of harvest was at hand.

And which of the above cases is represented by the image of the thirtyfold, the sixtyfold, the hundredfold? With Jesus, we have to say: we shall never know.

Under five general considerations, namely, the variety of soil, a quenched receptivity, the flash in the pan, the strangling collectivity, and receptivity, the rich expressions of the parable of the sower have yielded up their psychological meaning. What does the wealth of implications in Jesus' paradigm have to teach us for our psychotherapeutic practice?

The parable of the seed has a great deal to say that will not set well with many. But we must face the reality it underscores: it really is not a matter of "schools," groups, circles, methods — or even chiefly of the therapist. *Everything depends on the patient's inner predispositions,* as we have described them. This fact, which Jesus makes clear to us, is not easy for psychotherapeutic arrogance to stomach.

Carl Jung comes very close to putting his finger on this state of affairs when he places the "*autonomy of the unconscious*" at the center of all authentic psychotherapy. True psychotherapy can never be anything else but listening to, translating, and empathetically accompanying what the unconscious itself has to offer by way of expressions of, and possibilities for, the development of the human personality.

Chapter 5

Getting into Training

We have spoken of the will to be well, the courage for self-encounter, and the decisive prerequisites of each personal, individual conversion process, or receptivity, the willingness to receive. Now we come to the matter of *action* — getting into training, starting to "work out." Now the order of the day will be the actual practice of what has been recognized and experienced.

Talk, discussion, working things out in words, which can lead to fruitless altercation, as we know — all of this means little or nothing. It will sidetrack us, take us on an excursion into bald intellectualism. "In the beginning was the deed" is the watchword now.

Our new concern, however, from start to finish, is not a matter of doing unto others. It does not mean Bread for the World, diakonia, missionary assistance, or international assistance to so-called underdeveloped countries. Here the model paradigm for analysis is not the Good Samaritan, but as we have indicated, the key parable of the talents. We might entitle this parable the "Parable of a Return on an Investment" (Matt. 25:14–30; Luke 19:11–26). Its meaning is eminently psychotherapeutic. The various ways in which the different trustees deal with the capital entrusted to them decides their fate — their *utter, personal fate*.

As a theologian, of course, I am well aware that the parable of the talents is commonly ranged among the great biblical passages alleged to bear on what is called "eschatology," or the expectation of the Second Coming of Christ "at the end of days," including of course the so-called Last Judgment. To what extent we of the twentieth century ought still to be concerned with these particular cultural, dramatic, or, better, mythological representations is a question in my mind. Theology itself spans the broadest spectrum of attitudes toward these ancient representations, from total rejection to unyielding adherence. In other words it is precisely the "eschatological doctrine" of such passages that is in question even theologically. I am of the opinion that even if our parable were to refer unmistakably to the Last Judgment, it would by that very fact constitute first and foremost an indication for *action here and now*. After all, that last revelation can only be a product of the here and now. Of what use is it to me as a therapist to know the nature of the eschaton? And here I am speaking not only of the passage under consideration, but of any biblical locus alleged to contain eschatological information. Rather, my interest lies exclusively with Jesus' concrete statements of basic principle with regard to the achievement of an authentic, complete human life. Now, one of these basic statements, and a very special one, is at hand in the parable of the talents, which instructs me as a therapist concerning a return on the investment of one's own psychic potential.

Investment for a Return

The parable is the story of a return on an investment. A talent, which was a standard unit of weight in Jesus' day, was also the largest monetary unit of the time. A currency table lying before me from the year 1911 assigns it a value of some 5,000 marks. Thus it will be worth many times that amount in today's terms. The wholesaler in the parable is consigning a great deal of capital to subordinates of his whom he regards as particularly trustworthy. They are to put his money to work during the long period of his absence. They are certainly not expected simply to let it lie fallow. The merchant's trust, however, as he will at length learn, is requited in widely varying degrees.

The fate of the money corresponds precisely to the character of those dealing with it. The one to whom five talents have been entrusted fully justifies his employer's confidence. He has put his capital to work so cleverly that five more talents now lie in the treasury. The steward who has received two talents to invest has demonstrated the same fiscal dexterity. Their employer praises them to the skies. The third administrator, however, has done nothing at all with the talent consigned to him. He has simply stashed it away in what looked as if it might be a safe place, and now he simply hands it back to the astonished wholesaler. His justification? Why, he is not the guilty one, he explains to his employer. Who is, then? The employer himself! We need only listen to what the third steward says. The great capitalist is a "hard man," this underling knows, and so the latter is afraid. He had better really do nothing at all.

And the third steward becomes the principal dramatic figure of the parable. The storm bursts over his head. The employer recognizes his steward for what he is and excoriates him: he is evil, lazy, incapable, and useless. In particular the investor sees through his broker's insincerity. So he was afraid to lift a finger. He had no wish to rile so hard a taskmaster. Well, then, he ought to have walked to the bank with his talent and at least invested it at some interest! "Take this useless individual and throw him out in the dark. Let him howl. Let him gnash his teeth in anguish." And to the villain himself he says: "You have pronounced your own sentence."

Jesus adds: "The one who has nothing shall lose the rest as well." Obviously, from the construction of the sentence, "the one who has nothing" must have *something,* otherwise he would have literally nothing to lose, no "rest" of which he might be deprived. Rather he has "a hold on" nothing, he can earn nothing, he can manage nothing, he can take no responsibility. There is a difference, for example, between a religion of grace and a sacred disposition of passivity and pure taking. A religion of grace is not simply selfishness cranked up a notch to a selfishness about salvation. A religion of grace indeed proffers, even bestows, the capital to be invested. But we must exert ourselves in order to seize that capital and invest it. The same law of life is valid in

depth psychology. The unconscious will continually offer opportunities. But it is up to us to grasp them, integrate them, and
translate them into action.

Again and again, this proves to be too difficult a task for human beings. We need scarcely be surprised, then, to discover a
whole later tradition defending the third trustee in our parable.
After all, he is only sluggish and indolent, not evil! And the
wholesaler's sentence is reduced. We find this tendency crop-
ping up quite early in the history of the church. Eusebius, for
example, cites our text in his *Theophania,* in a commentary on a
parable in the *Gospel according to the Hebrews* in which a steward who has squandered his consignment with prostitutes and
flute players is thrown into prison; a second, who has gained a
magnificent return instead, is highly praised; and a third — the
one who has done nothing with the capital entrusted to him,
but simply handed it back — is only reprimanded.[1]

But Jesus does more than reprimand one who declines to
"take things too seriously" under the misapprehension that little things "aren't what it's all about." It is precisely the seemingly little things that Jesus takes so seriously, as our paradigm
demonstrates. It is a trustee's failure to take *one* talent seriously, his refusal to put it to work, as if after all nothing need
be done with just one talent, that calls his whole mode of existence into question. Similarly it is the *one* lost sheep that the
shepherd goes in search of so tirelessly. It is the *one* lost penny
that the housewife turns her house topsy-turvy to find. And
it is the *one* refusal to celebrate his brother's homecoming, on
the part of the elder brother who has always stayed home and
minded his father, that characterizes the elder brother's whole
being. Jesus' habit of appraising the whole on the basis of one
small part permeates all his speech and action, as we know.
Why? With what intrinsic justification?

In depth psychology, the small is the token of the great.
A seemingly trivial symptom may well reveal a patient's general condition — just as, in our parable, a steward's behavior
with a single talent betrayed the wholesale condition of his
soul. Money, whose symbolism, negative as well as positive, has
no limits, nevertheless always stands for libido in the broadest

sense: one's whole life energy, simply and as such. It represents
the *entire human being as such.* "Here. Take back the money
that you have given me," is *pregnant with meaning for depth
psychology:* "I really can't do a thing with myself. Just look
at me, anyway. I'm not worth a thing." The allegedly "only
lazy" steward has done nothing more nor less than *given himself up.* Jesus' parable is worthy of a basic, underlying role in
any anthropology. *No one has the right to give up!* This is the
message conveyed by the third figure in our parable. He is a
negative figure because he is inactive.

A particularly astonishing characteristic of Jesus' authentic
psychology comes to light here. No one has the right to give up.
One must *accept,* or learn to do so. This is not a mere conclusion
drawn by us from Jesus' words and actions. Jesus teaches this
principle explicitly, in inculcating its positive correlate: "The
one who pretends to be great will be brought low nonetheless";
and the other way around (Matt. 23:12). Thus those who think
nothing of themselves suddenly find themselves endowed with
magnificent potential. If we interpret Jesus rightly, then we see:

> Only when I accept myself do I have anything to do with
> the phenomenon that is called the grace and forgiveness
> *of God;* not an instant sooner.
>
> Whoever understands this presentation properly will
> not get the idea of raising the objection: That is indeed
> a dreadfully simple matter. Accepting yourself can be a
> bitter pill to swallow, at times extremely bitter.[2]

The imperative of self-acceptance is identical with the obligation to ensure that an investment generate at least some little
return. The inept steward of the single talent made no effort
whatever in this direction. In psychological terms, he gave up.
He was unable to accept himself as who he was — the administrator of a relatively small capital. But to fail to accept yourself
as who you are is tantamount to foregoing your own existence.
And "a lost life cannot be bought back at any price," Jesus
warns elsewhere (Mark 8:37).

Only too often do we encounter patients whose self-appraisal
is like the third steward's. "I'm not worth it. I can't do a

thing. I'm nothing." And they frequently add, "I might just as well end it all." To cite just one of many such instances: A young man came for therapy suffering from severe learning disorders. Academic catastrophe loomed. In his personal life, as well, he felt unloved and ignored, forced to play an outside role that was hateful to him. He felt unsuitable for everything under the sun. Even our analytic discussions at first totally failed to reach his abysmal inferiority complex. The analytic process was completely blocked. Inevitably, he "wasn't worth it." A dream heralded the turning point in his therapy. His mother was driving him somewhere in a car. (Ironically, in real life his mother had no driver's license.) Suddenly he was horrified to see that his mother had swerved into the entrance of an underground parking garage, where, he knew in a flash, she intended to park the car and abandon him. Not a moment too soon, he managed to leap from the car and make his way back up to the street. We addressed the interpretation of this dream. What had my client actually grasped in that last instant, that moment of truth? As he expressed it at the termination of his therapy, however limited his potential, he was not permitted to "park the car." He was not allowed to give up. And it all depended on him!

A man somewhat along in years, an excellent craftsman, but long disabled by illness, had decided that he must burden his wife no longer. He was no longer good for anything in any case. He had made three suicide attempts. In analysis, however, he became entirely aware that he still had capital to administer. In the meantime his wife fell seriously ill. Now it was he who became her prop and support. Thus his energy and sense of responsibility developed in an unforeseeable way. He was worthwhile after all.

The number of young people, especially, who like our third steward think of themselves as no longer capable of anything worthwhile and hack away at their wrists with more or less suicidal intent, at first astonishes. But it need not. A glance at the statistics will show the extremely rapid rise in suicides and attempted suicides. Why should our children and young people not be represented among the numbers of those who have surrendered, given up? We are fairly surrounded by stewards of the third category. At the same time, we must reflect that children and youth especially are frequently the victims of their environment. The real villains are to be sought elsewhere, especially among those charged with the upbringing of these children and youth.

Action

Capital is to be invested for a return, then. We are directed toward a goal, set in motion, called to action. Jesus' whole attitude is ordered to action. We began with his "Do you want to be well?" The matter to which we now turn our attention — the call to action — reflects this same emphasis on the will. We are dealing with an absolute basic here. It could scarcely have been otherwise. We have sensed it in the background of everything that we have seen so far. Here we could paraphrase Jesus' requirement: the name of the game is action! Each of the administrators receives an *assignment*. Jesus allows no "down time."

Once again analytic theory seconds Jesus' attitude. Analysis must be "done," even so-called academic analysis. There is no theoretical analysis. Analysis cannot simply be thought about.

Let us examine the basic component of analysis — practice — in greater depth. "What do you think of this?" Jesus asks. "A man had two sons. 'Go to work in the vineyard today,' he said to the elder. 'I don't want to,' the son responded. But he went. Meanwhile the man made the same request of his younger son. 'Gladly,' replied the latter. But he did not go. Now, which of the two sons did his father's bidding?" The first, Jesus' interlocutors rightly replied (Matt. 21:28–32). It is not obliging words that count. Action counts. With Jesus, two things are always in tandem: teaching and doing, hearing and doing, believing and doing, and so on.

"Jesus is objective," observes Ernst Bloch, in that drastic style of his, "especially when it comes to a lot of nonsense about a fully transcendent kingdom of heaven." Jesus will countenance no kind of "noninterference treaty" between the world of values to be defended and the dreary reality of our everyday lives.[3]

In his figure of the Good Samaritan, so plain and so sublime, Jesus has helped us to an awareness of the fact that action in the here and now, when necessary and required, is a spontaneous act of self-opening to an acknowledgment of ourselves in every aspect of our being. He has thrust the stubborn, burning thorn of conscience into our glib mountain of excuses. "Whatever you have done to any of these poorest brothers of mine, you have done to me" (Matt. 25:40).

Nor is all this emphasis on action an affair of principles, or legalism, or even outward scampering and bustling. It is a matter of spontaneous self-development. It is no coincidence that good land yields a rich harvest. A good tree cannot help bearing good fruit. And one who is "in the truth" also "does the truth."

This is why Jesus' call for action is only implicit. Jesus presupposes action, emphatically. It goes without saying that we shall act. Action is the spontaneous expression of that inner wholeness, that spiritual health, toward which an encounter with this psychotherapist thrusts us.

And vice versa: For Jesus, "Yes, you say it, but you don't do it," is the most devastating, most exposing reproach that can be hurled at a human being. It is the reproach he hurls at the doctors of the law and the Pharisees, at any hypocrisy at all, be it in personal, religious, or political affairs, be it in private life or in public (Matt. 23:3).

With a view to the action he calls for, Jesus also demands the highest degree of openness, pertinacity, goal orientation, and striving for that goal. Almost harshly, he declares: "One setting his hand to the plow and then looking back is unfit for the kingdom of God" (Luke 9:62).

But each of us is to plow our *own* furrow. Each individual is to invest the talent entrusted to that particular individual. Accordingly, the dynamic commitment demanded by Jesus is not essentially a general one, demanded first and foremost of a plurality, but an *individual* one. It must be *my* commitment. Precisely the therapeutic paradigm serving as our guide here, the parable of the talents, is an unambiguous expression of Jesus' clear-sightedness about the importance of the individual. Each of the stewards or trustees in the parable is consigned not the same, but pointedly *different capital* to be invested. Of each, accordingly, is demanded a very different return, in accordance with the differing potentialities of each. A survey of the differences among the various figures Jesus sketches throughout his parables, images, and other utterances would heighten this impression even further. However, the capital with which we are entrusted is not as loosely connected with ourselves as is a banknote in our pocket. It is always *ourselves* that is meant. In other words, we are preparing the final settlement of the entire account of our existence. Even analysis must not attempt to exceed reasonable goals, and thus overtax the patient. Rather it must see where the potential as well as the limits of each analysand lie and help this particular individual to go his or her *own* way.

To assist the individual to discover and appreciate his or her own spectrum of possibilities is an absolutely basic task of analytic therapy. How else might an analysand be expected to uncover the wherewithal to initiate his or her authentic action—the action that will be appropriate for this particular individual? In most therapy, the deeper ground of the neurotic complaint is precisely people's ignorance of their own measure. The difficulties impelling most persons to seek therapy are owing either to an exaggerated appraisal, or to an underestimation, of their own potential. The patient has succumbed either to "inflation"—illusions of grandeur—or to what we call inferiority complexes.

This is very far, we must say, from being an acknowledged, self-evident principle of the various currents of psychotherapy today. Freud could still say that, at bottom, psychotherapy is education to the truth against oneself—education to the truth that makes the individual "become what he might have become at best under the most favourable conditions."[4] This comes very close to what we have been saying. To be sure, Freud himself seems scarcely to have appreciated the full scope of the goal he sets, as we see from later scientific discussion. As for his successors, in the widest variety of approach, as well as for most other therapies practiced today, it must be said that their basic orientation, far from being the discovery of the inner self, is precisely an express or implied adaptation to collective standards and demands that may happen to be at hand. Jesus is certainly not in agreement with this. On the contrary, he is a walking protest, in word and deed, against blind adaptation or submission to the prevailing collectivity. We might better characterize his therapeutic goal as follows: adaptation in the correct manner (when the inner person assents) and non-adaptation in the correct manner (when the inner person can only distance itself from the prevailing collectivity). Which of the two alternatives an individual can or must embrace will ultimately be decided subjectively, in function of the substance and quality of the person concerned — who, after all, must inevitably go his or her own way, along the path found to be appropriate for that person's own being.

To set out boldly down our own path, to recognize the capital entrusted to us and in this sense to "become personality," is, as Jung once put it, "an act of the highest existential courage." Only in summoning up that highest existential courage shall we be able to do justice to the precious capital with which we have been entrusted: that restless demand within us, that inner moral thrust and impulse of ours, to become all that we can be.

> No one develops his personality at the behest of another. Nature has never been known to allow itself be imposed upon by well-meaning counsels. Only the causality of constraint moves nature, even human nature. Nothing changes without necessity, least of all the human personality. Only the keenest of needs will chase it out of doors.[5]

Jesus also makes it plain in his parable that, while the stewards act on the basis of trust, they also act under pressure of responsibility. Both trust and responsibility are required if an individual is to be set on the path to creative action. This is a well-nigh perfect description of the challenge with which psychotherapy must deal. Here too men and women are impelled, through pressure and through trust, to a new, constructive conduct vis-à-vis themselves and their environment. Only weighed down by a truly deep, pervasive burden of suffering, only when your chariot has gotten itself really stuck in the sand, only when you are tied down and it really hurts, can a fruitful analytic process begin.

At the same time, just as the honest stewards in the parable know that they have the support and trust of their master, so must it dawn on patients in analysis that they may lay hold of a *trust* in the benign, positively stimulating impulses and healing powers of the unconscious.

The third steward, the failed administrator, is missing both: the pressure that alone drives a person to deed, and trust. Thus no action and no results are forthcoming — only catastrophe. This same thing can happen in therapy, and we shall speak of this possibility in greater detail in the following section of this chapter. For the moment, however, let us examine a few actual instances of the awakening of a subject, at the hands of psychotherapy, to the responsible activity that we have seen Jesus so concerned to stress.

A law student had completed his course of studies brilliantly and had secured a candidacy for quite a high public office. Now he was really something. Now he had reached the top of the heap — only to discover that he stood in complete isolation in his personal life. He had always lived with his mother, who was well along in years now and who stuck to him unremittingly. Would he be able to do anything about this all but total isolation of his? Each and every step away from his crippling mother-attachment had to be discussed. Counsel and encouragement were easy, as abundant dream material was at hand. But action was another matter. Still, the young man managed to get up the courage to advertise for a marriage partner. But it was entirely out of the question that he should acknowledge any of the replies! I can't do that to my mother. And we encountered the most stubborn crisis of his long analysis. You *must answer*. If you can't do that, then we may as well stop. It isn't a matter of what may come of it. You owe it to *yourself*, to any hope you may have of achieving personal independence, to write responses to the replies that you have received. And every step toward responsibility for himself — moving out of his mother's house, laying the groundwork for an enduring relationship, and so on — was a veritable wrestling match with his all but stubborn indolence. But then came the breakthrough. It was not sudden, it was gradual. But it was a surprise. There he stood, happy to be alive, active, communicative, enterprising, creative. And the cost? Ah, that was all forgotten now.

A young student in a school of technology, certainly above average in intelligence, had seen his first year end in complete fiasco. Feeling the need of counsel, he came for therapy. His inner confusion was particularly evident in the almost overwhelming quantity of dream material at hand. It promptly emerged that he had taken up his technological studies only under pressure from a very ambitious father, who had placed the necessary financial wherewithal at his son's disposition specifically for this technological curriculum. The young man had even had to sign a contract the father had drawn up, guaranteeing the necessary funds only under a number of conditions. He had to continue with the course of studies chosen by his father. He had to submit regular financial and academic reports to his father. His father had the right to gather regular information on his progress in his studies from his teachers. Furthermore the son had the duty of spending at least one vacation a year with his father, who was divorced from his mother.

The turning point, the moment of inner clarity, was accompanied by a dream that made a deep impression on the analysand. He dreamed that an orchestra was holding its annual meeting and discussing its successes and failures over the past year. (My client actually played the French horn.) The president of the orchestra took the first violinist by the hand, presented her to the orchestra and audience, and announced that all of the credit for the success enjoyed by the orchestra over the course of the past year was due exclusively to her. We discussed the dream. It was like a bolt from the blue for the student. He recognized that he was off on the wrong foot in his studies. His gifts held the promise of success, yes. But it was not in the field of technology, he realized, that they lay, but in the realm of feeling, fantasy, and creative intuition, represented by the image of the concert mistress with the violin, receiving the public acknowledgment of the orchestra and the audience. Coming up out of his unconscious, this elucidation struck him so forcefully that he found the strength to rescind his father's humiliating, exploitative contract, change his curriculum, and work his way through school without his father's financial assistance. (Scholarships were practically unknown in his country.) Devoting himself to archeology and music, he succeeded in his studies. He had found his own way. He had discovered his own law.

Exams were in the offing for a student of the industrial sciences. He was a gifted young man, but psychosomatic disturbances — high blood pressure, heart problems, insomnia, and so on — made his work difficult and gave him feelings of insecurity. His dreams revealed a strong dependency on the authoritarian figure of his father, together with a great deal of inertia on his own part. He was lazy. He lacked initiative. In our discussion of the father problem, it appeared that the boy had taken up the industrial sciences only at the behest of his ambitious father, who, no academician himself, hoped at least to see his only son become one. So the student was not following his own way. He was following a path programmed by the father. This realization caused a liberation within him. He took a few weeks to think the matter over. On his return to analysis he was a changed person. He had managed to draw the conclusions suggested by his new insight. Over his father's protestations, he had given up his course of studies and been accepted as a trainee in the Bureau of Revenue. Now all his psychosomatic symptoms disappeared. Happy and content, he announced his engagement and looked forward to the future without anxiety. As we see, one's "own way" can readily enough lead to the Bureau of Revenue.

The Inflated Failure

The failed steward in our paradigm is lazy. But his indolence is only a symptom. We have not yet discovered its cause in terms of depth psychology. What psychic problem constitutes the causality of his behavior? Why does the third steward simply hand his talent back unused?

It is not mere speculation to conclude that he felt handicapped. And he *is* disadvantaged by comparison with the other two stewards. But this appraisal originated with his master, who knows with whom he is dealing and what he can expect of him. The steward himself is not prepared to accept this realistic judgment. He is without the courage for self-encounter that was our concern in chapter 3. His false pride, his shadow, will not allow him to acknowledge who he really is — a person of somewhat limited capabilities, but therefore a person of capabilities. What is expressing itself within him is what we today know as the celebrated, the infamous, inferiority complex.

Now, it is our experience in psychotherapy that, to the inferiority complex of an individual, unbeknownst to that individual, an "inflation" corresponds — a sense of exaggerated worth, as we have explained above. And it can be outrageous.

This false feeling goes hand in hand with a false appraisal of reality. Unconsciously, the sufferer is constantly ruled by extraneous potentialities and standards, which, however, totally overtax the individual who adopts them. We downright believe ourselves to be someone special, and thus must achieve so very much, something huge, even something altogether out of the ordinary. The unlimited demands we now place on ourselves can of course not be met. So we sink back into our crippling feelings of inferiority. And the vicious cycle recurs. The upshot? Instead of something special, nothing at all materializes — exactly as with the third steward in Jesus' parable.

The inflated failure will, however, by no means admit that this sterile behavior is a matter of personal responsibility. A person with an inferiority complex will say, and think, that it is others who are guilty of all these failures. In the parable it is the merchant himself who is to blame. After all, it is he who has decided how many talents each of his underlings should receive. In real life it is the elements of one's environment — family, upbringing, and the like — that must bear the onus of the blame. A seventy-year-old woman explained to me, apropos of her various kinds of failure over the course of a long life, that it was all because her parents neglected to tell her about the birds and the bees!

When all is said and done, the inflated failure of our parable, the third candidate, is full of inconsolable self-pity. He beats back his failure, keeping it at arm's length lest it touch himself. He is but the innocent victim of brutal exploitation, he feels. What we have, then, is a complex of inferiority feelings, exaggerated self-appraisal, and self-pity. And so the question poses itself: How does Jesus deal with this problem? What might we be able to learn from Jesus' *modus procedendi,* perhaps even for our therapy? But before we attempt a detailed answer, let us see how the "third steward" looks in actual therapy.

An extremely depressive young man, unable to work, and with his life on the brink of total disaster, came with a desperate plea for help. A discussion of his background brought to light that he and a number of younger siblings had been fathered by a foreigner who lived with their mother but refused to marry her. He was an illegitimate child, then, and that fact dogged his every social relationship. In his dreams, however, he was of wondrous birth. He was the Babe in the Manger, he was an avatar, a descent of a divine spirit! Thus the illegitimate child became the divine child. A handicapping birth became an identification with gods and heroes.

Again we see feelings of inferiority offset by an exaggerated feeling of worth. The dreamer had to be brought to the realization that illegitimate birth is neither a shame nor an honor, but the assignment of a task to be performed in his everyday life. In his specific case this would be the task of having an earnest confrontation with his father. He must call the latter's attention to his responsibility as the father of a family to marry the mother or otherwise legitimate his children. Financial considerations were at stake, however, and the patient was very far from daring to risk his father's ill will. Thus he never became capable of exploiting his full capabilities and simply continued his complaining, his self-pity, and, especially, that fantastic self-appraisal of his.

A patient particularly in need of help will suddenly discover a calling to be a psychotherapist. Of course! What else? We meet with this phenomenon frequently in analysis. Jung himself called attention to it. A young Englishman once sat before me, flaccid and lethargic, complaining of impotence. He was not, for that matter, exactly a brilliant success otherwise. I asked him what he wanted to do with his life. His answer surprised me. "Sit in your chair." Ah, he wanted to become a psychotherapist!

Another "Of course! What else?" case: A young woman came to me in excruciating marriage difficulties. The story she told was not the more or less usual history, but one of a failed relationship obviously stemming exclusively from the side of the husband, who emerged as a person of extraordinary cruelty. He was also a drug addict. I asked my patient how he obtained the wherewithal to purchase drugs. "Oh, he works here," she responded. And just what did he do here? Why, he was a marriage counselor.

But why all the fuss? Are we not subjecting our inflated failure to a bit of overexposure? Scarcely. The "third steward" represents a very particular danger and menace, both in individual relationships and for society at large. Their failure drives them to such a towering self-appraisal that they not only blame others, they avenge themselves on them. Jesus was right on target from a psychological viewpoint when he represented the third steward as aggressive. Insolently, shamelessly, the latter makes the owner a "hard master," as we have seen. It is he, and not the hapless steward, who is responsible for all of his trustee's failures!

We encounter the third steward on the highway, driving as aggressively as he can and thereby causing a crisis situation, then executing precisely the wrong maneuver and causing an accident. We meet him in sex murderers, who are too shifty and inhibited to establish normal relations with women, so now they avenge themselves on them by murdering a few. We meet the third steward in commercial life, where so many swindlers and cheaters answer his description. And of course we meet our inflated failure in political life: it has been asked, with good reason, how world history would have gone had Napoleon been four inches taller, or Wilhelm II not had a withered arm. Alfred Adler in particular has called attention to this "organ inferiority" problem, and suggested that some compensatory functionality may have set to work to offset a crippled sense of self-worth.

The creation of the great historical *Feindbilder*, or enemy projections, those victims of the anathemas of masses and peoples, is to an enormous extent the product of this sort of inflation. Jesus' description of this personality type is simply excellent. We need not be shocked at the Lord's seemingly inhumane tirade in the town square. It is a simple matter of Jesus' correct grasp of the total psychic situation. The words he places in the mouth of the hoodwinked employer are entirely appropriate: "You have judged yourself out of your own mouth." That is, with your haughty, high-flying aggressivity, you have identified yourself as an inflated failure, as useless as you are dangerous.

A Matter of Training

Looking back on our parable as a whole, let us ask ourselves what it has to teach us. As in the preceding paradigms, so also in the present one, with its universally valid principle of capital to be invested for a return, we are furnished with a basic guide for psychotherapeutic treatment. After all, no rational insight, no rational explanation will lead to psychic healing. Only one's own responsible action, in answer to the demands of the psyche itself, will lead to this therapeutic goal. Responsibility for our own behavior cannot be acquired overnight, of course. It is a habit, and habits are acquired through the exercise of their acts — in the present instance, through daily goal-directed activity. There is no escaping it: we simply have to "get into training." Jung used the image of a spiral staircase. You work your way up, step by step, constantly circling the central, supporting pillar of the whole installation.

The training to which we refer has nothing whatever in common with the insertion into the patient's daily round of some "occupational therapy" or other, generally something not calling for a great deal of personal commitment. No, by training we mean the accomplishment of the *specific task the psyche assigns* in information welling up out of the unconscious. But this is always precisely the task the patient has fled, to take refuge in this or that neurosis. It will be precisely here, then, that we shall be able to distinguish the patient who is willing to develop into a genuine, healthy person from the lazy, but therefore all the more swaggering, failure. The separate steps to be taken are often difficult, and may turn out to be too much to ask of the third steward. That is the nitty-gritty of analytical therapy, and everything depends on it. At the same time this insight should function as a damper on any notion of psychotherapy as the magical wonder-drug that will heal and regulate anything in an instant.

Eight weeks before examination time a student came for treatment of her learning and concentration difficulties. She was disappointed that she could not be admitted into treatment at once. She had really hoped that between now and exam time she could put all her difficulties behind her and be able to walk into the exams perfectly fit.

Let us look at just a few examples of the extreme importance of the attention to minutiae that is required by this crucial element we have called getting into training. And let us see this in cases involving different sorts of neuroses. To help a female patient get into training, it is often a decisive step to be able to bring her to a degree of self-respect that will enable her to say no. The psyche demands this, since the patient makes her affirmative response to every imaginable unjustifiable demand responsible for her psychic exhaustion. One patient dreamed she was driving a car without doors. All along the trip, people constantly got in and out. Of course the passengers were non-paying, but she drove blithely on. The client was a woman with an acute sense of social commitment. Although married and the mother of several children, she was constantly being asked to rescue situations that in actuality had only arisen because of the indifference of others in her circle of acquaintances. She was being used and exploited, but she put up with it. She knew something was wrong: "I'm dead on my feet, but I still can't say no." She had to have a new motto: "I can say no!" — hammer it in, and think of it as working like a mantra. Any further appeal to her over-availability was to be measured by this new maxim. She succeeded in a relatively short time. Most importantly, she came to realize that she had been confusing genuine social commitment with *ego-weakness* and indecisiveness.

The following example is typical of our experiences with patients complaining of *neurotic depression*. Only too often it very quickly becomes clear that their seeming lack of energy — which according to them is what makes them incapable of doing any work — far from being due to an actual lack of libido, or vital energy as such, is actually a matter of the stagnation or blockage of that libido, that energy. The patient's psyche is like a too shallow dam. A dam will drive its turbines only if the water is able to build up the necessary pressure. Otherwise it will simply lap uselessly over the edge, trickle down the side, and actually initiate processes of decay. Translating this back into psychological terms: in the case of very many individuals suffering from depression, the basic difficulty is that their upbringing, or their own sluggishness, maims their available energies.

This is the lot, for example, of so many women who marry after attending the university. They think that they can settle down into the closely confined existence of the everyday housewife. Just such a woman, after her very first therapy session, had the following dream. She dreamed that she was a schoolgirl again, on her first day at school. "The teacher welcomed us, and began his talk by telling us that it was a very special day today: the hundredth birthday of Gotthold Ephraim Lessing." Our discussion of this dream naturally centered on the question of what Lessing might symbolize for her. She knew practically nothing of either the author or his works. I began to try to extract some of her hidden memories. Recollections gradually emerged. There were dramas, like *Nathan the Wise* or *Minna von Barnhelm*. She had been especially impressed by Lessing's *The Education of the Human Race*. Then there was Immanuel Kant's concept of enlightenment, based on humanity's emergence from self-inflicted ignorance. The patient determined to occupy herself with Lessing's reflections on these matters more in depth at home. In the next session she reported another dream. Once more she sat as a pupil in the classroom, where the teacher was quizzing the class. All the pupils had their hands in the air except her and one other girl, whose name she remembered. We discussed the dream. Now my client recalled that the other girl had been an especially lazy, indifferent pupil.

Ah, so this was how her shadow figure looked. My client had become comfortable and indifferent herself, and she was reflecting her feelings about this in her dream. It became clear to her that she was actually anything but overburdened. Now she must *do* something, she realized, and do it energetically. The "doing" with which she proposed to begin was a mental activity, but one that would also reflect a stronger commitment to her family. She had to "go into training" to do this. In other words she had to go at her new activity step by step. But as she progressed in her "doing," her depressions subsided and a new joy dawned in her life.

Depressions can present a complicated problem, and there are instances in which even the seemingly most banal training tools are not to be despised. A pencil, for example! A strikingly pretty young woman was escorted to therapy by her desperate young husband. She was the victim of constant depression. She wept inconsolably and interminably. The most affectionate initiatives on the part of her husband failed even to bring a smile to her face. The following state of affairs came to light. The young man, who labored under a severe mother-attachment, had actually been reared by a domineering aunt. Only with difficulty had the young bride succeeded in untangling her husband from his aunt, as it were. But now she had entered unconsciously into competition with the aunt and had learned to dominate the young man even more completely than the aunt had. How? By means of her constant heartache and affliction, which called forth such great attention and consideration on the part of her husband. The fact that what had deprived her of all joy in life was her own neurotic behavior, which had boomeranged, was just as unconscious to her as its instrumentality in winning the control game with the aunt.

But then came a moment of truth. The young woman recognized her unconsciously guided behavior as being purely and simply a neurotic ploy — an artful power play in the game for the control of another. Desperately she asked, "But what can I do to stop needing a power play?" The answer: Get yourself another voice. Indeed her tone was insufferable — whining, pitiful, pleading. I suggested she sit down with her husband in the evening on a regular basis and read aloud something of interest to them both. While doing so, she would make every effort to use a normal, matter-of-fact tone of voice. Her husband would sit alongside her with a pencil in his hand — and make his presence felt whenever she fell into her old, plaintive whine. This common endeavor, affectionately undertaken and pursued, would launch their "training" in better partnership. The effort succeeded.

This *doing,* this training, likewise occupies center stage in the treatment of *compulsion neuroses.* Indeed it is of a particular importance here. The causal factors in compulsion syndromes — for example, a washing compulsion, a bathroom compulsion, an attention compulsion, and so on — are relatively easy to discover. Both anamnesis and dream material (the latter being relatively skimpy in these cases) as a rule point pretty clearly to some developmental deficiency, usually dating from early childhood. Evidently, then, treatment will center on an attempt to effectuate an extensive restructuring of the character. And of course this will demand, once again, an approach consisting of very difficult, small steps, one after another. But the basic direction the therapy will have to take will be indicated the moment it becomes clear that the foundation of all of these compulsion symptoms is a fear originating with feelings of guilt. The purpose of the compulsion ritual is to seize this fear and tie it down. But a vicious circle comes into play. Answer the demands of your compulsions and you are indeed delivered from your fear for the moment. But nothing within you has changed. You are still in the clutches of your neurosis. In fact the demands of the agonizing ritual will now have a tendency to grow exponentially, so that you will have to adopt more and more rituals and practice them more and more often and intently to keep your fear under some semblance of control. Try to resist the compulsions, of course, and the fear will appear to increase ad infinitum. And back you go to your compulsions. No intellectual elucidation of the causes and course of the neurosis will be of any avail, as experience shows.

Obviously, then, therapy will have the task of helping the sufferer break out of the vicious circle in question by means of a training in an altogether different kind of *doing*. But it must be a kind of doing that will confront the patient again and again with the question of how much fear he or she is ready and willing to accept. In this fashion, instead of merely warding off this fear by various neurotic means, the sufferer learns, step by step, to accept and conquer it. Once the patient has accomplished this, he or she will have the critical, pivotal experience of watching the fear actually diminish, instead of merely being suspended. And since nothing succeeds like success, this will be accompanied by a healing encouragement, a strengthening.

All of this is verified in actual case histories. One patient suffered from a compulsion syndrome so cruel that it threatened to cripple her personal life in every respect. If she went to the bathroom she had to use three or four rolls of toilet paper, and the plumber had had to be called repeatedly when the toilet became stopped up. Perhaps the most painful aspect of her cleansing ritual was her compulsion to dip her hands in a whole series of concentrated disinfectants. Morning ablutions, along with her dressing ceremonial, lasted so long that her youngest child was usually late for school, and now he was full of fears as well. Her husband could hardly go to work at all, as he was constantly needed at home as a controlling factor. In the patient's prehistory lurked a prudish, sexophobic upbringing, guilt feelings stemming from an adultery she had almost committed, self-incrimination with respect to masturbation, and the tormenting memory of an intended, but not actually secured, abortion.

All compulsion symptoms to a certain extent represent symbolic attempts at self-purification. Naturally the patient's background was the subject of discussion in her therapy sessions, but her compulsion rituals were ironclad. For example, she had to cleanse herself exactly twenty times whenever she had finished using the toilet. "Starting today," I suggested, "let's try it with nineteen." "I'll be afraid," was the immediate response. "You must learn to bear this little bit of fear," I rejoined. She tried. Yes, she could bear this little bit of fear. And so, by degrees — intentionally, lest the patient become too frightened — we arrived at a reasonable number of cleansings. At the same time we scheduled similar exercises, for dressing, hand-washing, and

so on. And of course the more the analysand learned to antic-
ipate a certain amount of fear and make up her mind to bear
it, the less there was to bear. Now for the first time she could
do some paid work, in a group of other women — a visible sign
of her success. This had truly been a therapy by baby steps, a
therapy of getting out and doing, and it had not even taken a
terribly large number of sessions.

A case of *impotence:* A student involved in a live-in relationship came to me in desperation. He had become hopelessly
impotent. An exploration of his circumstances, and the state of
his unconscious, disclosed a very phlegmatic young man, anything but enterprising and without any wish to become so. In
a word he was lazy. His lover seemed discouraged to the point
of wishing to withdraw from the relationship. Thus deprived
of his last crutch, he decided to come for therapy. He was
promptly confronted with the painful insight that his impotence
was merely a specific symptom of the general impotence of his
attitude toward life. He never bothered to get out of bed before eleven o'clock in the morning. He attended one lecture a
week at the university and otherwise passed the day in idleness
and ennui. He scarcely had any dreams. Further discussion was
curtailed. Nothing more was said of his specific symptom. Instead I suggested that he buy an alarm clock at once, set it for
eight o'clock, and rise at that hour each morning. This would
be a first step. He managed it. Then he was to reflect on how
he might schedule a constructive division of his day and week.
Here there was some hesitation at first, but then some obvious
interest. By the time of the very next session he was able to
present quite a respectable, orderly schedule for his daily activity, and he promised to keep to it. Of course the matter of
perseverance in this new beginning was the subject of constant
discussion, which proved to be most helpful. Six weeks later
the young man was no longer recognizable. He had managed to
hold to his own program. The amusingly charming signal that
his therapy could be terminated came in the form of a midnight
phone call. The only thing the analyst could hear in the receiver
was, "I can do it! I can do it!"

By way of conclusion, let us observe that the "doing" that is demanded of us may consist in *not* doing something. What the psyche requires of us in terms of our training may be a resolute abstention from, for example, an unwholesome overactivity, an inefficient, unproductive overtaxing of ourselves in our particular line of work, or indeed an activity of any sort that has been causing us unhealthful stress. Let us have one final example.

A completely overextended psychologist, her health a shambles, came to therapy with the following dream to relate. She had dreamed that she had had car trouble. She took the car to a garage. The mechanic went over it most carefully, then said with a laugh that it was no wonder a car like that would break down. And he invited the dreamer to come over and have a look. To her astonishment, her car had two gas pedals, one in the usual position and the other just behind the driver's seat. As the pedals were connected, when she depressed the one the other would function as well. Just how this was accomplished will forever remain the secret of the dream, but the fact remains that when our psychologist stepped on the gas the motor got twice as much as it could use. In other words she was expending twice the needed amount of energy for whatever she wished to accomplish. Her dream had created a particularly forceful image of what we mean by "burning your candle at both ends."

When Jesus begs us so urgently to *do* something, and not merely talk about it, he is not demanding mindless, overtaxing bustle. He is asking for an organic activity, one that emerges from our inner wholeness and issues in the same. Once more, then, he provides us with a consummate model of the permanent focus of the entire therapeutic endeavor: to make sick persons, incapable of appropriate activity, well — to help them to a constructive series of actions that will shape their lives in joyful responsibility.

Chapter 6

Humane Image
of the Human Being

Demosthenes Savramis writes that it has been two thousand years since a totally corrupt society crucified Jesus because he dared to tell it that it was corrupt, because his good news threatened to devastate a society that lived by the dehumanization of the human being. Out of fear of the "new human being," whom Jesus himself pre-lived, Jewish society killed Jesus. It had grasped that, after all, the new human being can blast to pieces that form of society that obstructs the humanization of the human being. Our own task, Savramis continues, is to ensure that the humanization of the human being, inaugurated with Jesus, forges ahead. Jesus desires to lead us out of our calamitous, salvationless situation — all of us, individuals and societies, today as yesterday. And the motto of his inchoative radical alteration of the world is: "The Humanization of the Human Being."[1]

But the humanization of the human being is also the ultimate goal of analytical psychotherapy, which strives to render neurotic cripples, their psyches in shreds, as fully effective and as normal as they can possibly become. If this process of humanization is to be legitimate, we must never cease to learn from the conception of the human being as we find it with Jesus.

To speak of the "humanization of the human being" may sound paradoxical, even tautological. Actually this is far from

116

being the case. To be sure, the formula is calculated to spark attention. But as a matter of fact the conception of the human being that we commonly maintain, that we have in our minds, that we deal and work with as if it were a self-evidence, is far from being always humane, indeed even human. It very frequently fails to reach the human level and acquires a subhuman character instead. The humanization of the conception "human being," therefore, is definitely a task of the present, and one as urgent as it will be difficult. After all, working against its progressive accomplishment it has all of those civil and societal forms, together with the many individuals whose interests are bound up with such forms, that unquestionably would all be blown to pieces should the desire in question meet with so much as a modest materialization. And as these structures and individuals evidently feel that materialization subconsciously, they heap violence on violence in the hope of being able to continue to stage their subhuman shadow plays a little longer.

With precious few exceptions, church and theology fail to cooperate in the humanization of the human being as they might. When they want to talk about the human being, they start right in on God again. After all, we hear (and it sounds so plausible!), only from a point of departure in God will human beings be able to understand themselves genuinely as human beings. And so we learn a great deal about the humanity of God, but little, when all is said and done, about the human being.

Let us ask first, then, which ideologically conditioned misconceptions of the essence of the human being and human psyche stand against an authentic concept of that human being. Only in this way shall we be able to arrive at a correct appreciation of what Jesus as psychotherapist has to say to us in this regard.

Misconceptions of the Human Being

Fairly beside himself with frustration, Jesus once cried out: "What sort of twisted people are you, anyway? Without a bit of trust! How long do you expect me to be able to put up with you?" (Matt. 17:17). Among the "twisted people" whom, in

Jesus' judgment, one cannot tolerate for long, are three typical kinds today, corresponding respectively to three false constructions of the concept "human being."

First, we have the champions of a *mechanistic model of the human being*. Freud himself introduced mechanicism into depth psychology. In Freud's conceptualization, the human motor is kept running by all sorts of "mechanisms." We have drive mechanisms, defense mechanisms, and so on and so on. First of all, we have to say, such a conceptuality is completely unscientific. It is as if we tried to apply the basic categories of physics to biology, or those of aesthetics to mathematics, or said that logic is bound up with emotions, and so on. The human being is not a machine. It is improper, then, and utterly unscientific, to speak of its "mechanisms." Secondly, even apart from their unscientific quality, the ultimate mechanistic orientation or *Weltanschauung* underlying these concepts is an encumbrance with which the concept "human being" likewise refuses to be saddled. Freud was a child of his time in this respect. Willy-nilly, he was an advocate of the ideological tenets of Karl Marx. All religion was neurosis for Freud. Indeed, there were no absolute values of any kind. Freud was a pioneering genius, but he never succeeded in divesting himself of an image of the human being that was no image of the human being at all. It was a mechanistic caricature.

The great modern founder of mechanistic thought is René Descartes. Descartes actually attempted to create an ethics *more geometrico* — "in geometrical form." The "father of modern philosophy" thought of the human being as a little machine, functioning as part of that gigantic machine, the cosmos. All parts coupled, all gears meshed. Of course Descartes found himself unable to suppress the weird suspicion that the whole mighty motor had been started up by some goblin who wanted to make fools of us. But ever since Descartes, in ever changing guise, the Cartesian, mechanistic mindset has prevailed.

Today, Karl Marx and the conceptual world of industrialization constitute a battering ram that makes Descartes's pale theory seem like a child's fillip. Together they have procured the all but universal acceptance of mechanistic thinking and a mechanistic understanding of the human being. It would be a sheer waste of words to present a critique of this model of the human being. It is no model of the human being at all. But it is simply incomprehensible that the majority of psychologists and depth psychologists today should prattle on about human mechanisms, and even discover new ones, utterly innocent of any critical spirit, and actually believe that this is the way you are scientific. The whole pitiful image of a mechanistic psyche only shows us once more that one of the ways in which the Freudian school demonstrates its authenticity is by prolonging, indeed intensifying, its master's shadow.

Again among the "twisted people" whom, according to Jesus, one cannot long endure, are to be found today those who can only conjure up a *"human being from below,"* as they like to say. This time the prejudices are biological. The "human being from below" is a kind of higher beast, so that a comparison with beasts, and a constant appeal to what may be learned from experiments on animals, pervades the whole literature.

But surely biologists far overstep their bounds when they leap from animal experiments directly to a sketch of the conception of the human being. For example, biologists often experiment on rats. Now, if human beings were rats, biologists would not be overstepping their bounds in applying their findings to human beings. A rat psychology, says Russell Jacoby, fits the human being only when a throttling world has metamorphosed men and women themselves into rats.[2] The great modern forebear of this biologistic perception is of course Charles Darwin, whose theory of evolution leads from the amoeba to the human being in a homogenous, unbroken chain. The magic word "evolution" supplies the abiding guarantee that this syncopated, biologistic concept of the human being will maintain and extend its currency.

Today, however, a number of biologists and medical researchers have begun to question this evolutionary biologism. The life work of Adolf Portmann is particularly worthy of attention in this respect.[3] Among the more recent researchers in this area we may cite Erich Blechschmidt, who gives the coup de grace to this maimed model of the human being "from below" (could one manage to take the latter seriously in the first place). In the abortion debate, for example, we heard again and again that the "little blood clot" in the first three months of gestation is "of course not a human being yet." And yet Portmann had already demonstrated that a specifically human development is initiated from the moment ovum and sperm meet. Blechschmidt puts it very plainly: "The ever recurring question why and when a human 'becomes a human being' is misstated from the start. A human being does not 'become.' A human being *is*. A human being behaves as a human being from the very first." Even the one-celled human zygote is an "individual organism," Blechschmidt shows us. All of its ontogenetic development, from conception to birth, is the development of what is already present.[4] To set forth the argumentation underlying Blechfeld's inescapable conclusions would take us too far afield. Suffice it to say that "the question in which month of ontogenesis a human being comes to be may no longer be regarded as a question. A human being is a human being from start to finish." But the biologistic mindset blunders obliviously ahead. After all, the "human being from below" is an ideology, and an ideology will think whatever it has decided to think. It regards thinking "from the bottom up" a great, revolutionary leap forward.

Still another basic perversion today is the compulsion to manufacture an unconditionally *value-free* conception of the essence of the human being. This attitude harmonizes extraordinarily well with the other two distortions that we have examined, mechanicism and biological positivism. The value-free standpoint is often expressed so crudely that it betrays its advocates' de facto atheism. Such is the case with Bernhard Grzimek, for example, the famous friend of the beasts.[5] (Animals suffer too, do they not? Who cares about them?) Grzimek's picture of God is most primitive. God is the "Great Mother," giving and giving, maintaining all things in order, preventing all mischief and guaranteeing the victory of right. Such a perception is of course pollyannaism in the extreme, as we should have long since learned from Feuerbach's critique of religion. There is far too little evidence in the world of any such guarantor of the universal welfare for Grzimek to be regarded anything but an atheist. What advocate of such a primitive representation could be called anything else? Grzimek's grand lucubrations evince one thing: that their champion has long since ceased to bother to do any thinking about the hapless object of his cavalier negligence. This is what is typical and dangerous in this sort of positivism, which is the ideology dominating the intellectual scene today. In all questions of value it is infantile, in the psychological sense: it knows nothing, but it produces magnificent explanations of that about which it knows nothing. Then other ignorant thinkers jump on the bandwagon.

We have made no attempt to present an exhaustive survey of the hostile matrix in which the human being's self-reflection must be carried out today. The three "twisted models" that we have sketched in such broad strokes have two things in common: their basic orientation, and their conquest of practically the whole of depth psychology. Freud himself is the powerful initiator of the process. Marx, Darwin, and Freud are a trio, historically as well as objectively. Freud transfers to psychology what Darwin and Marx say in other disciplines. And thus a catastrophe bursts over the head of depth psychology in its very cradle. There has never been a time when it has been exempt from victimization by mechanicism, biologism, and positivism. Indeed, so extensively and comprehensively is it imbued with these hostile influences that Wolfgang Kretschmer can solemnly proclaim: if there is anything on the face of the earth that will never be able to serve as the foundation of a modern conceptualization of the human being, it is psychoanalysis.

But the three unhappy influences sketched above have done more than merely permeate and conquer psychology. They have produced what we might call a *psychologistic model of the human being.* Descartes and Feuerbach, Darwin and Marx, were theoreticians. By contrast, the psychologistic image of the human being is a dangerous, destructive, dehumanizing force. It is not a theory, but a violent bid for power. In politics and economics, in the schools, in the factory, at the office, in the university, in the arts, it says, "Might makes right," and its hegemony goes all but unchallenged.

The church's image of the human being is not invulnerable
to this violent assault. Bland and impotent, it is the product
of an anthropology as nerveless as it is ancient. The church
has always been able to say a great deal about God, grace, and
the afterlife. It has had very little to say about the human
being. The void left by the church and its theology has been
eagerly and noisily filled, especially over the course of recent
decades, by anyone pretending to have anything at all to say
about the essence of the human being. Indeed, as we have seen,
we have had to live with inadequate, dangerous descriptions of
that essence. Here the churches have by and large contented
themselves with voicing a feeble protest. Nor must we overlook
the fact that they have allowed their doctrines to flow with the
currents of the time. This was the quest for "relevancy," we were
told, while in actuality the churches were undermining their very
existence. The culmination of this trend is that contemporary
psychologism has carved out a niche for itself in the churches
themselves.

A comprehensive, integrated, genuinely humane model of the
human being has never prevailed in Western thought. When it
has seemed to, at one time or another in history, it has never
been long in showing its true colors. Only relatively recently,
in Jung's analytical psychology, have we been presented with
the opportunity to adopt just such a comprehensive theoretical
model and practice it.

And the opportunities furnished us by analytical psychology
for a comprehensive understanding of what it is to be human
set us squarely on the threshold of an unexpected, electrifying
discovery. It now dawns on us that we at last have just such
a comprehensive, integrated, objective understanding of the human being available and ready to hand. This image, this model,
is already present to us in Jesus. Jesus has demonstrated it. He
has personally lived it.[6] Thus the disheartening history of the
subhuman images of the human being, apart from the manifold
projections of each respective age, becomes only the story of
an ongoing apostasy. Our new discovery of Jesus' image of the
human being is actually only a rediscovery. And this rediscovery of ours includes a rediscovery of the fact that Jesus' image

of the human being is a genuinely humane one — indeed, in its determining, basic traits, *the* genuinely humane one.

Then no authentic modern psychotherapy can do without it. And yet our modern psychotherapy is still very far from implementing even the base lines of Jesus' model.

How do these base lines present themselves in Jesus' model of the human being, especially in his manner of dealing with human beings and his understanding of individuals?

Total Projection-Withdrawal

Primitive human beings, who have not yet "come to themselves" — who have not yet acquired a critical awareness that can take its distance from its object — experience themselves not actually as they are, but rather as they are reflected in the reactions of their environment. They identify with these reactions. For example, they experience their fears or their guilt feelings in the eerie rustling of the wind in the trees, or the interpretation they happen to make of the expressions on the faces of the persons around them. They live in a state of more or less exclusive projection. This was the state of consciousness prevailing in Jesus' environment. Over against this primitive level of consciousness he lays the foundation for a new one: "What makes a person unclean is not what that person takes in from outside, but what comes out of that person from inside" (Mark 7:15). Thus Jesus radically cancels the principle of self-identity by identification with the external. And he thereby takes a first, enormous step forward in the history of the generation of human consciousness. In Jesus' terms, it is the "inner" condition of the psyche that is crucial. It is the psyche's own qualities, its own measure of its responsibility for itself, that count. The dynamic moves from within to without, and never the other way.

This turning point in the history of human awareness has had decisive consequences. The precepts of ritual purification, for example, which dominated the whole of life, have been invalidated once and for all. "You sanctimonious ones! Your plates and cups sparkle like the sun, while you yourselves are full of rotting garbage" (Matt. 23:25). A perfectly clean, repeatedly washed plate or cup is used by Jesus to stand for the whole, detailed cleansing ritual, which he recognizes as the vehicle of a confident projection of an inner purity that does not actually exist. This is the attitude of a person who focuses on the easier, outer task in order to avoid having to come to grips with the more difficult, inner one. Once this projection is recognized as such, the divorce between the sacred and the profane is cancelled forever, to be replaced with a universal openness for all future time. The correct direction of authentic human responsibility, from within to without, is no longer obstructed by walls of separation between the within and the without.

The sabbath prescriptions — to cite just one example from the endless lists of actions "permitted" and actions "forbidden" — now lose their significance. Jesus' great leap forward in human awareness has divested of all importance anything that would seem to legitimate the substitution of an outward deed for an inward attitude. Indeed the very concept of a righteousness based on works crumbles, resting as it has on the same foundation. Jesus makes such a concept of righteousness look ridiculous. What a consuming zeal! How you shudder at the thought of depriving God of so much as the tithe of condiments that is his due! And yet by taking such colossal account of the minuscule you only convert sense into nonsense, for you thereupon take but minuscule account of the colossal. You disregard what is truly important. You "strain out the gnat and gulp down the camel."

Jesus' image is lapidary. Dispensing with the spirit of casuistry altogether, our new plane of existence simply invokes the principle: "Either you plant a good tree and the fruit will be good, or you plant a rotten tree and the fruit will be rotten. You know the tree by the fruit" (Matt. 12:33).

Jesus has transcended this plane of existence, a level of being expressed and fulfilled in projections alone. It is scarcely a relic of history, however. The act of its surmounting is more than a once-for-all historical occurrence effectuated by Jesus. While this inferior level of acting and existence occupies a low rung indeed on the ladder of human psychic development, it is constantly with us nonetheless. It is a basic manner of acting today, from which the ascent to a more conscious level must be managed ever and again. The only variable is the historical phenomenology of the projections throughout the ages. Today we no longer have cleanliness rituals and sabbath prescriptions to dismantle. But the essential kernel of this task remains: to overthrow our habit of evaluating ourselves, and others, by mere outward standards — standards of industrial, commercial, political, or other achievement. The moment we can no longer "do" anything we become worthless, to ourselves as to others. The achievement compulsion is the modern secular counterpart of the religion of doing and righteousness of works that Jesus repudiates. Furthermore, from Jesus' standpoint this immense obsession with doing, this inability to discover a standard of value anywhere but in growth quotas, can only be appraised as a projection. Today's human beings, these mighty doers, have failed to achieve that inner development demanded by Jesus two thousand years ago that would have raised them to the level of the authentic, humane human being. Indeed they project their self-validation in their so-called accomplishments, in their world of exteriority, more than ever before.

What Jesus demands is the withdrawal of this projection. He does so in the name of a genuinely humane human existence and being. Jesus, we see, is the everlasting modern.

This is why it seemed so crucial to Jesus to eradicate the projections human beings lay on one another's backs. To this end he shows us our fellow human being in a new light. *Our fellow human being is our neighbor.* To be sure, we shall at once have to listen to the objection that the Old Testament had already spoken of "neighbor," and "love of neighbor." Jesus, we shall hear it explained, merely took the concept of neighbor from the Old Testament, which had handed it down to him, and "radicalized" it. The imprecision of these determinations, however, is tantamount to their untruth. The fact is that Jesus raised the concept of neighbor to an altogether new level. He invested it with an altogether new quality and timber.

The concept of neighbor in Jesus' time, and the received ethical practice with regard to this concept, is by no means as clear-cut as we may be inclined to suppose. The question put

to Jesus by the doctor of the law, "And who is my neighbor?"
(Luke 10:29), was an arrogant, aggressive assault, a question
posed in a spirit of ignorant self-assurance. It was intended
to embarrass Jesus, to compromise him, and thus provoke a
confrontation of an altogether radical order. But Jesus took up
the challenge, and created, in the figure of the Good Samaritan,
a new symbol of the quality of authentic humanness, one that
burst asunder the entire mental and societal framework of his
milieu, indeed that revolutionized human relations across the
board. What is it in Jesus' new image that emerges as so broadly
revolutionary?

The ancient Jewish concept of neighbor was actually an altogether particularized one. An insight into its narrowness and
rigid circumscription can perhaps best be afforded through a
consideration of the human categories it did *not* include. Its
basic criterion was membership in the people of the covenant.
The Romans, for example, were certainly not "my neighbor,"
any more than were other foreigners or *goyim*. Nor of course
were tax collectors and "sinners," that is, the unrighteous —
not to mention prostitutes and adulteresses. (Adulter*ers* went
literally unmentioned.) A special anathema, however, by comparison with which all previous exclusions from the category of
neighbor pale to insignificance, lay on the peoples of Samaria.
These had come under a general societal proscription analogous
to that of the untouchables or *pariah*s of India. (Jesus' tale
of a Samaritan as the ideal protagonist of the good, we see,
was a biting, intentionally explosive provocation of his environment.) And then there were the many successive gradations
of the quality of neighbor, complete with a full-blown drum-
tight casuistry to determine who might still be acknowledged
as quasi-neighbors. Women and children fell into this last category, along with widows, orphans, and the elderly. But ... what
about, for instance, male Jews expelled from the community by
reason of illness, such as lepers? Are *they* still "neighbor"? An
interesting question. And the list of "cases" is endless.

But let us not be so naive as to think that it was only Judaism that proceeded with such inhumanity and particularism
when it came to the concept of neighbor and its practice. To

the Romans, the Roman alone was neighbor, of course, the *civis Romanus.* To the Greeks the Greek was neighbor, but not the barbarian. To the Indians a member of one's own caste was the only neighbor. And so on, down to our present day. That the concept of neighbor, despite Jesus, has not yet fully divested itself of its primordial particularism and spirit of reservation is abundantly attested by the class struggle and the racism of our own day.

What conclusion is to be drawn? What phenomenon or fact fashioned these countless persons, actually one another's fellow human beings, into one another's seeming *non-neighbors?* The ineluctable answer: any given group inevitably heaped upon, projected upon, foreign groups and classifications any particular unconscious inferiorities of their own. Thus these other groups and classifications were to be despised and contemned. This is unmistakably clear from all that we have seen, especially from our basic discussion of the essence of projection in the context of the paradigm of the Pharisee and the tax collector.

So what does Jesus do? He exposes the whole phenomenon of disparagement, degradation, and exclusion from the human community of the non-neighbor for what it is: a gigantic, cruel transferral of one's own inferiorities to the supposed responsibility of another. Only the withdrawal of such a transferral, which Jesus calls *doing penance,* at last makes the face of my fellow human being to shine upon my inner life: There's my neighbor!

How was Jesus able to do that? Certainly not by virtue of his radicalization of a concept allegedly long since at hand. No quantum leap has ever taken place by virtue of an intellectual radicalization. No, Jesus was able to revolutionize the concept of neighbor by as it were *becoming* "Samaritan" neighbor personally to each and all. He projected no unconscious inferiorities of his own upon the human beings around him. Thus he could accept them as they were. He *had* no unconscious inferiorities of his own that would have blurred his vision. Thus the Jesus-event itself becomes the great, one-hundred-eighty-degree turn from particularism in all its forms to a universalism that embraces the world and humanity.

Inasmuch as it extends to neighbor and stranger alike, friend and enemy, this universalism is for Jesus an expression of authentic perfection. It expresses the specific perfection of his picture of God. God makes the sun to dawn on the evil and on the good, he says. God makes it rain on the just and on the unjust (Matt. 5:45). God makes no distinctions among persons, and we must be guided by that model. Consequently we must pronounce no degrading, excluding, dehumanizing judgments, which of course is the essence of projection. Rather we should look on each and every one as a genuine neighbor. Jesus' invitation to perfection, which, as we see, is perfectly understandable psychologically as well, applies to us: "Be perfect, as your Father in heaven is perfect" (Matt. 5:48).

In this same connection, we must emphatically call attention to Jesus' cancellation of that particular projection that in such singular fashion has determined *women's lot* down to our very day. In the harsh, rigid patriarchate of Jesus' milieu women were degraded to the status of non-neighbor, as we have indicated. They were counted inferior beings, quick to lie and to gossip, designing, unreliable, and impure. They must under no circumstances place their hands on the holy scriptures. For adultery they were stoned, while their partners went free. The entire primitive mentality that pervades androcentric antiquity is at hand in Judaism as well, crass and unbroken, loveless and hard. Above all, women were never to be forgiven for the alleged fact that it was a woman's disobedience to God that once brought sin into the world, corrupting the whole human race, as indeed the fathers of the church would continue to say.

What is being projected here? Men in the time of Jesus maintained no psychic relationship whatever with women, or indeed with the feminine as such. The case of women is not just one more instance of the case of one's neighbor, which we have just discussed and which would have been problematic enough. No, women are altogether unique partners to men, with their own specific life modality, and that modality remained closed to men. Neither, for that matter, did men have any comprehension of women's self-fulfillment or concrete life expressions, to say nothing of specific feminine life-values such as receptivity, acceptance, openness, empathetic appraisal and judgment of reality, spontaneity, nonrational address to concrete reality, and so on.

Men's own unshakable standards for themselves are after all so completely different — the drive to achieve, the rationality, the legal mind-set. Feminine values, measured by these standards, in Jesus' milieu as in any purely male-dominated culture, appeared as visionary, vague, and illogical, hence surely counterfeit. Let a conflict arise between the male and female life modalities and men know but one reaction: they grow *angry* and depreciate women psychologically and morally. They fail to notice, of course, that in reality they are *only projecting on women their own incapacity* to understand or even surmise the feminine. Women appear to men in the light in which *they* see women — a false light. On such uneven ground there can obviously be no common progress.

Jesus falls completely outside this framework. He never becomes angry with women, as is evident from the accounts. He never even criticizes them, let alone disparage them. He ignores all walls of separation, such as that prohibiting a man from so much as greeting a woman on the street.

Instead, women are actually his disciples, accompanying him on his journeys and supporting him out of what they possess, as we learn from the gospel texts. Free and unconstrained, Jesus consorts with women without hesitation or prejudice. He enters their houses unconcerned. He defends them when they are the victims of harshness or contempt. The adulteress who is about to be stoned to death suddenly finds herself rescued. "Let the one among you who is without sin throw the first stone at her" (John 8:7). This pericope, whose textual formulation is attested only rather late in the formation of the canon, is certainly authentic in its tone and import.

One must not eviscerate these connections. Jesus is not merely "friendly toward women too." Rather one must recognize the *basic* meaning of these encounters: Jesus grasps both the values of women's being and the mode of their reactions, hence also the values of feminine being as such.

The Greek woman from Syrophoenicia, already mentioned in another context, provokes a bit of a conflict between herself and Jesus when she reminds him of the puppies that at any rate get the crumbs that fall from the table. Thus she counters Jesus' rejection of her. Instead of growing angry, Jesus examines her argument objectively and accepts it (Matt. 15:21–28). Who knows, perhaps it is she who will be in Jesus' mind the day he creates the parable in which the tenacious widow gets the best of the unjust judge by dint of her sheer persistence. Likewise Jesus understands the woman with the hemorrhage, who thinks she need only "grasp" Jesus (Matt. 9:20–22). Again he understands the woman who attempts to express her attitude toward him with a concrete, extravagant gift of expensive ointment, and who actually anoints him with it (Matt. 26:6–13). Jesus has an understanding of the typical feminine reaction, consisting of spontaneous, nonrational expressions of feeling and concrete address.

Where does this understanding come from? How is it to be explained? Jesus is the first male in world history not to be bound by one-sided masculine standards and value judgments. *In his person, Jesus has broken through the one-sidedness of a male-centered age and transcended it.* Feminine existential values and modes of reaction have become interiorly accessible to this male. Thus he represents in his person a synthesis of both of these erstwhile questionable modes of managing one's existence. We are not merely taking a plausible position here. In his words and in his deeds, Jesus demonstrates the objectivity of our assertions. And suddenly we see why Jesus, in contrast to his male contemporaries, does not feel a need to disparage women, even interiorly: *Jesus harbors none of the unconscious predispositions for a negative projection upon women.* On the contrary, in his behavior as in his speech, he develops the richness of masculine and feminine values alike, thereby laying the groundwork for an integral model of the human being for all time to come.

Once More: Projection Today

We have already spoken of projection withdrawal, especially in a context of our chapter on the courage for self-encounter. Having broadened our insights a great deal in the foregoing paragraphs, we have come to a point where it will be appropriate to illustrate them once more with material from current practice. The road to the humane human being, the subject of our new chapter, in psychotherapeutic practice runs by way of conscientization and withdrawal of one's projections. But as we have just seen, the road that leads to our fellow human being, whether simply as neighbor or as sexual partner, is the very same, that of the dismantling of our unconscious projections. Thus Jesus' behavior in this respect stands as a model and orientation for all time, especially for psychotherapeutic treatment.

It is bootless to search outside ourselves for the solution to an inner problem. The recognition and conquest of the problems we have within us must occur within us. Jesus recognized projection for what it was, especially where the victim is our neighbor, women, or for that matter anyone's partner of the opposite sex. It is an "internal affair."

A pilot for a leading commercial airline had had a shattering experience. His psychic disturbances had now manifested themselves in a way that threatened his profession. He had initiated the landing maneuver in a large commercial jet. Suddenly his view of the instrument panel was completely blocked by the larger-than-life image of his twenty-year-old daughter. Only with the greatest difficulty had he managed to overcome the shock and land the plane. He came for therapy. He thought that it was simply a matter of nervous tension, and that therapy might be just the thing for the "stronger nerves" he needed to solve this "professional problem" of his. However, his analytical treatment very quickly made it clear that he was faced with a set of severe problems in his relationship with his daughter. In other words he had an incest problem on his hands. As we see, an unconscious inner set of problems can be so intensely projected to the outside that it actually becomes *physically visible*. Not surprisingly, then, an inner restructuring was needed in order to remove the outer symptom that was such a threat to the pilot and to others. The papers call it human error. We call it an inner psychic disturbance.

A young married man came for therapy. He was so full of

fears that he could not sleep. Only on weekends, when there was no work the next day, was he partially free of his fears and able to get a night's sleep. He was an excellent worker, yet he suffered from secret feelings of inferiority. His worst torment was the question of what his supervisor might think of him. As ill luck would have it, he worked in the same office as his supervisor, and hence had to suffer the additional discomfort of feeling himself to be under constant observation. His answers to a series of questions established that his insecurity was the product of a faulty relationship with his parents in childhood, which had partially hindered the development of the masculine element of his psyche. To be sure, this had nothing to do with his supervisor. Nevertheless the latter had become the projection figure upon whom the patient had transferred his inner fears. The patient comprehended and accepted the situation on an intellectual level, yet the fears remained. A purely intellectual elucidation, no matter how accurate and to the point, has no effect on the unconscious. But then came the following dream. The patient dreamed he broke into his supervisor's fortress-like house by night to eavesdrop. He hoped to hear what the supervisor might actually say or think about him. After a great deal of exertion he reached the living room, which he found to be ablaze with light. There, to his surprise, he saw his supervisor simply playing ping-pong with his children.

This dream was a burst of enlightenment. Thunderstruck, my patient realized he had not the slightest reason to trouble himself about what his supervisor might think of him. The supervisor had concerns of his own. Besides, he was a kind, humane person, and surely not likely to harbor dark thoughts. On the other hand, my client had every reason to take his own inner development in hand. Now that the heavy burden of this projection had been withdrawn, the supervisor no longer came into the analytic picture, and the patient's developmental deficiency could be corrected working from the inside out. His analysis was terminated after the following dream. The supervisor invited the patient to a fine restaurant, where the restaurateur expressed his satisfaction at seeing the two of them together after such a long while, and they both had a good time.

The supervisor had not changed, but the patient had. He had grown up. He had acquired a measure of maturity through the process of dealing with his problem, which included the strenuous effort of a withdrawal of his projections on the supervisor. At this point the symptoms that had impelled him to seek therapy disappeared of themselves. This is an altogether typical illustration of one of the effects of projection withdrawal. An intimidating, authoritarian figure is transformed into a kindly superior and colleague, that is to say, into a fellow human being, a neighbor.

Following are two further illustrations of the fact that, today as in the time of Jesus, a relationship of partnership cannot be lived to the full without the withdrawal of unconscious projections. A young woman came for therapy as a last resort. Every day, the whole day, she wept. All joy had fled from her life. She could give no reason for these constant tears of hers — except that perhaps she did not feel that her husband took her seriously enough. But on questioning she had to admit that her husband actually made every imaginable effort to cheer her up. Then she had a dream. She dreamt she saw her husband huffing and puffing his way up the side of a mountain. On his back was perched ... herself, clinging to his neck and letting herself be toted. My question to the dreamer was: What would you advise a woman in that situation? My client: Get off and walk. My rejoinder: Well, get off and walk.

From this point on, the young woman's treatment consisted mainly in seeking out the concrete ways in which she was allowing her husband to carry her in some way, and how she might become independent and responsible instead. The wife had originally regarded her marital partnership requiring the husband to carry each and every burden, including herself, while she simply let herself be carried. And the tears? The tears were the tears of a little child who had lost her mother. Her new partner had not been able to take care of simply everything for her, as her real mother had when she was very small. She had to withdraw this projection. Only when her husband had been delivered from the mother image that she had unconsciously slapped on him did he become visible to her in his proper role of partner and spouse.

The following case is in a way just the opposite of the one above. A patient complained everlastingly of his wife. She was frigid, sexually unresponsive. His advances were wasted, despite a careful study of the latest in sexology and the great lengths to which he went to meet her expectations. Confidentially she was not actually very feminine. Careful questioning yielded no answers. Then a dream came like a blow. The patient dreamed he was walking along a street with his wife. They came to a big cow standing in the way. They both knew that the cow must be slaughtered if they were to continue their common journey. The dreamer, however, did not know how the cow might be slaughtered. His wife, on the other hand, explained reassuringly that she knew about these things, and would see to the matter. Upon being apprised that the cow in the way was a mother symbol, the patient admitted that he had been a very spoiled little mama's boy whose mother had taken care to gratify his every whim. Now he was projecting this unconscious picture of woman as a spoiling mother on all women, especially his wife. His wife had not met his expectations, however, and he felt constantly frustrated with her. But instead of looking for the basic reason in himself and his immature attitude toward his marriage partner, he thought he could unload the burden of his dissatisfaction on his wife. It was *her* lack of understanding, *her* faulty development that caused his problems. But his dream spoke another language. It was actually his mother-attachment that blocked the common path of the couple's development. He himself, he had dreamed, had not even been in a position to remove this obstruction. Rather it had been the much-maligned wife who alone could remove the barrier. And indeed in real life the wife declined to play the maternal role expected of her. She continued to regard her husband as her partner and to challenge him to function as such. Both partners, especially the husband, came to accept these complex unconscious associations, and their marriage relationship improved remarkably.

In each of the four cases just cited, as in all similar cases, human beings become more companionable, less biased, more considerate, more friendly, more "together," more closely related — in other words, they become more humane — when their projections no longer conceal their actual substance, and therefore no longer divide them. We learn this from Jesus' manner of dealing with persons. That manner, we see, is abidingly modern.

Development of Functions

With the withdrawal of projections, of which we have just spoken, a great developmental leap forward has been taken in the direction of our goal, the humane personality. Projection withdrawal produces a shock. For the first time, I have seen myself as I really am. My habitual, extraneous camouflaging has been stripped away, and I can no longer make others responsible for my own shortcomings. I have come to a moment of truth. The question of who I am is no longer theoretical. It is a practical, existential question now, and I pose it with adamantine realism. *Now* when I ask myself who I am, what do I see? I see a human being in no position whatever to manage the reality confronting me. I lack the necessary psychic apparatus.

What do we mean by the necessary psychic apparatus? This time let us begin with a concrete case from modern therapeutic practice.

A young technologist, with a doctorate in his science and a very important job, came to my office in the greatest desperation. The rearing of his only son, about eleven, was causing himself and his wife the most unpleasant difficulties. The main problem was the youngster's toilet training, which of course should have been completed long ago. The boy not only wet his pants, he messed them, even during the day and even in school, to the point where no one was willing to sit next to him. Manifold efforts at toilet training had failed. An exploration, or close questioning, of the father, together with an analysis of his dreams, showed him to be a very parent-attached man, who, as such men often do, had married a considerably older woman — a mother figure. He was in no position, then, to assume the role either of husband or of father. I questioned him about his relationship with his son. Did he spend time with him? Did they do things together? The answer: "No. Look, he's smelly!"

What do we see here? We see a father who simply cannot go on because he has at his disposition none of the necessary *instruments for performance* of the task incumbent on him — in psychological terminology, the necessary *functions*. Good will has abounded in the past, but his response to the question about his relationship with his son shows that even the good will has capitulated. Here is a professional success, a scientist much esteemed by his colleagues, who is a total failure in his private life. We should not be far from the mark were we to say that we are dealing with a psychic cripple — someone lacking the most important tools for the management of reality in its manifold challenges. Our scientist has developed one function: thinking, the intellectual function. He has succeeded in his professional life, then, for in technology the proper instrument is the intellectual function. But in shaping his marriage or understanding his son he is hopelessly incompetent. And there are other functions missing. Here we have a drastic instance of an individual's total helplessness by reason of the underdevelopment of his psychic functions.

Would Jesus have accepted his own helplessness in this situation? Far from it. In Jesus we encounter an exemplary, *exceptionally rich development of the manifold functions*. That is, in Jesus we have an outstanding example of the development of an approach to reality in its totality. We see this first of all from the fact that Jesus had no set method, no schema, no hard and fast behavior pattern, no monotonous, one-track series of reactions. On the contrary, Jesus exercised the capacity to meet everyone on the latter's own terms. Were his questioners Pharisees, with their crafty intellectual traps? No matter, he "stopped their mouths," as Luther translates, with his disarming superiority. And how did he come by this superiority? Indisputably, by virtue of a highly developed *feeling function*.

By "feeling" here we do not mean what we understand in the colloquial use of the word — emotion and emotivity, sentimentality, the friendly slap on the shoulder, and so on. Feeling, here, is rather the capacity for a creative molding of reality in conformity with an ultimate, constructive outlook on values. Feeling in its psychological meaning has nothing in common with softness and sweetness. Feeling is what you have when you overleap intellectual processes and find the answer directly, with a definition and final certitude that renders further discussion superfluous. Feeling is creative. It goes into operation, with determination and a sense of decisiveness, in any matter of the ultimate management or organization of life — therefore when all purely intellectual explaining has done its best and fallen silent. For example, Jesus' host, as well as the other guests around the room, whisper behind their hands: look at that fellow, behaving so casually and being so friendly with that notorious woman of the town. Jesus' reaction is to tell them all the story of the two insolvent debtors. Their generous creditor cancels both their debts, one a very big one, the other a very small one. Then Jesus leaves it to the cavillers to decide which of the two will bear their benefactor more affection in future. Of course there is only one answer. "Surely the one to whom more is remitted" (Luke 7:36–50). And suddenly a new level of value judgment materializes, where intellectual judgments will be insufficient and where new opportunities for life and living will be created instead. And so Jesus concludes: Yes, absolutely correct — and this is exactly what is going on in this woman. So much has been forgiven her, bestowed on her, that her grateful love swells beyond all bounds. Addressing the woman herself, Jesus vouches for her conversion to a new way of life: "Your trust has rescued you. Go in peace." And there was no more argumentation.

We have caught a glimpse of Jesus' feeling function at work. No one else in the room saw anything but a whore, weeping for the life that had passed her by. Their judgment was clear, and that judgment would stand — so they thought. Jesus saw a suffering, searching human being. And he turned to her, creating new opportunities within her for her life. This is precisely the essence of the feeling functions, which we can learn from Jesus as from no one else. And now we are in a position to draw a basic conclusion whose relevance we dare not underestimate. As we have seen, Jesus' feeling function is at the dynamic center of his personality. But this is the case with any personality. What is the effect on the personality as a whole of this central, dynamic position of the feeling function? Precisely as a dynamizing sense of values, precisely as a value-creating function radiating from the mid-point of the personality, the feeling function also develops any further functions that will be required for translating its values into concrete reality. This is the case with Jesus, and this is the case with anyone. As broadly and as extensively as it can, *the feeling function brings the other functions of the psyche both to materialization and to fruitfulness.*

It is characteristic of these central functions, for example, to be able to *behold the inner being* of persons and things spontaneously and directly. Infallibly the feeling function pierces straight through all superficialities, strips them away, allows no mere symptoms to confuse or distract it, and thrusts undeviatingly to the core of a being. We have had repeated occasion to observe Jesus' capacity for gazing into the depths of the human heart. We see this faculty at work especially where persons who find themselves confronted with Jesus at once become directly aware of their unconscious shadow. Let us consider just one more example (Mark 2:1–12). Four men are carrying a sick man, described in the gospel as gouty or crippled, on a litter. They come to the house in which Jesus is addressing a large number of people. The crowd is so thick that they cannot make their way to him. But the four are resourceful. They simply dismantle part of the roof, a thing easily done in the East, and lower the stretcher practically in Jesus' lap. Now something most unexpected occurs. Jesus pronounces no healing word, as the patient and everyone else expect him to do. He heals the cripple indeed, but after his own fashion. He simultaneously publicizes and heals the sufferer's real malady. "Your sins are forgiven," he says. Jesus has intuitively perceived that the patient's real affliction is something more profound than his sore legs. The obvious physical disease is a mere symptom. But as he speaks a healing word of his own choosing over the sick body, we see that his diagnosis must have been correct, for the symptom disappears of itself. The crowd can scarcely have had any notion of the secret, profound, effective interchange transpiring between Jesus and the sick man. Indeed, despite all the efforts of scientific interpretation, the question of the effectiveness and manner of operation of the intuitive function remains to this day one of the greatest mysteries of the human psyche.

An alert, operational feeling function is likewise exemplified in Jesus' *capacity to see reality concretely, to allow it to achieve all of its concrete individuality, and to render it accessible to each and all.* Everywhere he goes, Jesus sees need and suffering that others are only too ready to take for granted and overlook. Often enough he gets involved without even being asked. Bodily illnesses are just as important to him as are maladies of the soul. He perceives the whole of reality, all of which constitutes his area of endeavor: the flowers and the birds, children and old men, women and the poor — everything within his field of vision and operation. This sense of the practical is also demonstrated by the manner of his proclamation. All things little and great become the vehicle of ultimate meaning. He observes the woman baking bread, the farmer plowing his field, children playing in the road, a fisherman catching fish, shopkeepers vending their wares, and so on. They all become the illustrative vessels of his proclamation. Indeed, how else could all persons, whatever their level of formation or age of life, have so easily understood the essential meaning of Jesus' assertions, down to our very day?

Jesus' *intellectual capacities* bear a special stamp, placing them far beyond the general norm. He is not the bringer of a new doctrine or metaphysics, as for example a Buddha, nor is he a rational lawgiver, as a Moses or a Muhammad. At the midpoint of his activity, as we have shown, are will and action — that is, the practical command of life. At the same time he has just the right word to say, be it for friend or be it for foe. The cunning challenges, the trick questions of his intellectually warped adversaries are exposed. His opponents are checkmated. And it is his adversaries who must bear the brunt of his sharp-honed intellectual argumentation. We feel safe in asserting, however, that when he elects to express what is most typical of him he directly engages his feeling, his penetrating insight into the essence of things, along with his gift of a sharp, concrete grasp of reality.

Looking back on what we have seen, we may now say that the image of the human being proposed by Jesus, in his person as in his activity, is one that is comprehensively humane. First of all, Jesus evidently has a great many tools at his disposition for recognizing, seizing upon, and creatively molding his surrounding reality. We see a *rich image of existential capacities* unfolding before us. Jesus is anything but riveted to, dependent on, a single function. In dealing with patients I like to compare psychic reality with a large house. We can really live in this house, I explain, only if we have the right key to each room. The fewer the keys, the smaller the usable living space. The keys are our psychic functions, installed in us in all their potential wealth so that we may be able to command our surrounding reality in a variety of ways. But these capacities by no means all stand at our disposition. We do not develop them. Hence we can make no use of them. Our outlook remains narrow and circumscribed. The main culprit in the process of this shrivelling of the *humanum* is a collective development that has persuaded human beings that there is nothing on the face of the universe that they cannot bring to materialization through the use of their flawlessly functioning thought or intellect. This persuasion habituates them to a crippling limitation. Why should we then be surprised that our most elementary life relationships simply refuse to function?

The man with the "smelly kid" was a good example. He stood helpless before the problem of his son's upbringing. He too owned but one key, the thinking key, which opened the door to his professional field beautifully, but which, unfortunately, did not fit the children's room. The key to the children's room had to be cut in analysis. The problem of the functions arises in nearly any analysis, and must absolutely be regarded as a matter for therapeutic treatment, not because any theory prescribes this, but because the unconscious itself protests the crippling lopsidedness of the patient's functions, making use of his or her dreams to drive them to broadening and development.

This was the urgent problem besetting the man with the little boy. His psyche was driving him to broaden his functions. He was a past master at thinking. But threats and punishment had had no effect on the lad, as his father was forced to admit. Now he had to be reminded that he was, after all, the child's father, and I asked him to try to think what a child might expect from a father. And because his son's smelliness had provoked such an unfatherly alienation on his part, I suggested that perhaps the youngster smelled because he had already tried every other way of attracting his father's attention and now was using a means his father couldn't ignore. The smelliness was advertising. The father had to understand this advertising and accept it as such. Then the symptom in question would no longer be necessary and would doubtless disappear of itself. His homework for the next session would be to consider what sort of activity a father might undertake together with a youngster his son's age. To my surprise, in the next session my client told of having started a physical training program with his son over the weekend and of how enthusiastic the boy had been. Fired by his first success, the father now came up with a steady series of new suggestions — soccer, kite-flying, hikes, and the like. These too were implemented. In an incredible six weeks' time the youngster was "clean" and a father-son relationship was in place! This had been possible only because the father had broadened and extended his psychic capacities.

I should like to cite two more brief examples of how the psyche's call for a broadening of its capacities is issued in dreams. A patient dreamed she owned a beautiful big house, several stories high. To her great wonderment, however, she had to live only in a pair of little attic rooms, the only furnished space in the house. My client was a very rationally orientated older woman, with little developed feeling. Even at this age of life the unconscious did not neglect to call for a psychic expansion, however, and my client responded to the call with some degree of success. The garret motif, expressed here by the little attic rooms, often appears where the intellectual function is heavily dominant in the global personality framework.

Another patient who had great problems in developing his feeling had the following dream. He was eating a square loaf of bread, baked in four distinct layers. He picked up the first layer and ate it. He picked up the second and ate it. The third, however, was not readily detachable from the fourth, so he reached for a knife. Suddenly he heard a voice: "Patience!

Don't go hacking at it! Wait. It'll come loose by itself." A square stands for totality, as does the number four, the number of layers in the square loaf. The reference will be to the totality of the psychic functions, as Jung has shown. The dream warns the dreamer against precipitancy in their development, however, as the psychic functions can be developed neither piecemeal nor violently, as one might slice something off with a knife. The functions must grow organically, and be constantly exercised, in order to develop. Not for nothing, we might add, do we hear Jesus using pictures of trees, seed to be sown, and so on, to symbolize organic, but not too hasty, growth, all bound up with his emphatic, thematic call to action and practice.

In this chapter we have spoken briefly of the integration of functions, as we find it with Jesus and as our task for today. Apart from our examination of the problem in a context of Jesus' speech and actions, we have presented the problem mainly in one concrete case, a question of upbringing and rearing. In actual fact we are dealing with a problem of inexhaustible dimensions. Confronted today with problems of ecology, of humane behavior toward nature and beast, problems of partnership, society, and so on, on whose solution nothing less than our survival depends, we honestly find ourselves completely helpless. Even technologically and intellectually guided attempts to find new solutions have all produced nothing but disappointment. Why one blunder after another? Because we are collectively mired in the very predicament that we have seen dog the efforts of individuals in this chapter. Even with the macrocosm, we try to open the *whole* of reality with the only key we have ever perfected, intellectual thought. And of course our search for a solution, our attempts to develop a genuinely humane mental attitude, founders, just as with our scientist and his smelly youngster. Perhaps our environment must stink in our nostrils still more before we finally see ourselves compelled to transcend our own psychic crippling and develop more adequate psychic capabilities — and of course not just for our own selfish advantage. Only then shall we become truly humane human beings. "Be converted!" Jesus admonishes us.

Developing Our Consciousness

However, not even the development of our psychic functions will automatically guarantee the becoming of the humane human being whose model is held out to us by Jesus. We are all familiar with a horrendous example of this insufficiency from modern history. Before the eyes of all the world, an interplay of the most varied and highly developed spiritual capacities was set in motion to realize a product that made the world hold its breath. The work had been conceived by the most towering use of the intuition. The most incisive thinking had conceived the necessary laws for the implementation of this intuition. Now a gigantic industry supplied the necessary technological requirements, and a devout man of the highest ethical principles put the final product to work "for the good of humanity," christening it the "fulfillment of Jesus' sermon on the mount." We refer, of course, to the atomic bomb.

Developed functions? This is how they can look. Functions are necessary instruments for acquiring a command of life, but they scarcely guarantee its humane command. They are first and foremost *value-free faculties*. As a consequence the value of their engagement with reality will always depend on *who* engages them, on what authentically humane qualities distinguish the one applying and using them. Only the genuinely humane human being can rightly engage these instruments.

And so we must pose our question a third time. Who or what is humane? Looking back over what we have seen, we may remind ourselves that the first qualification for the status of *humanum* was the withdrawal of projections. Next we called it genuinely humane to develop, insofar as possible, all of the psychic capacities found to be installed in the human being by way of potential functionality. But the case of the atomic bomb has shown us that even when we have succeeded in developing those capacities, we have not developed them humanely. The consciousness that has made use of them was still narrowly and lopsidedly masculine. We have already shown that Jesus' consciousness integrated both modes of being, masculine and feminine. Jesus' consciousness was broad and creative, his con-

sciousness was humane, precisely in this, that he exhibited just
as penetrating an understanding of feminine values as of masculine; that he even co-assumed them organically into his own
male consciousness; that even his image of God is saturated
with feminine values, and that just on that account his image is
universally valid. But we have also shown the seamy side of the
daily reality in which Jesus lived and moved — the fact that he
stood alone in a world stamped with purely masculine values.
And we may add that in the two millennia that have elapsed
since these phenomena came to pass, the further development of
the human psyche, far from following the direction indicated by
Jesus, actually stamped the total consciousness of that psyche
even more profoundly with its determining masculine values,
especially through the world of technology.

But where half of humanity, the feminine half, is not only dis-
regarded in the minting of that humanity, but in some measure
directly disparaged as inferior, no humane image of the human
being can materialize. It would be a tragic error to imagine
that today, naturally, everything has changed. We need only
peruse the sensational study of Elisabeth Beck-Gernsheim, *Der
geschlechtsspezifische Arbeitsmarkt,* which she wrote as part of a
special research project conducted by the University of Munich.[7]
Beck-Gernsheim shows that the typical feminine manner of performing a task blocks upward mobility in the various occupations and professions. Precisely all that has been developed,
fostered, and instilled in the female psyche as the essentially
feminine manner of working disqualifies women in the operational procedures of today's workplace. It not only collides with
the structure of those operational procedures; it irritates men,
rendering them startlingly inclined to relegate women to the
lower professions and occupations. And what precisely are some
of the typical aspects of the "feminine manner" of executing a
project? A person-oriented approach, a personal, disinterested
concern and solicitude for the success of the project, a disincli-
nation for elbowing tactics, a lack of interest in purely abstract
aspects of a task or job.

Thus we have reached the point — if indeed we have not always been here — where women "who are not burdened with

family tasks generally encounter greater professional difficulties, generally enjoy fewer and less promising opportunities, than do their male counterparts." Whenever the perceived value of a particular profession or occupation within the overall economic and political process changes, you can be sure, and the record shows this, that "the upgraded component of the activity in question will develop into a male activity, while the downgraded component will be relegated to the status of a female activity." Conversely, "when female participation in an occupation or profession rises, the social status of that profession or occupation will tend to fall." We must say, then, at the risk of simplifying a bit, that the case is ever the same: a woman's handicap is being a woman. How could it be otherwise in an ever more preponderantly male-centered civilization? The author is well aware that the solid wall of sex-specific professions is today suffering some initial breaches. But the outcome is still in question. Suppose both sexes were indeed one day to have access to all professions and occupations. Must today's rigid, antagonistic, competitive tension forever continue to prevail between sex differences and objective tasks?

Jesus' project of a humanization of the general consciousness has not made a great deal of progress, then, in the intervening millennia. Thus it is scarcely to be wondered at that the imperious world of masculine consciousness, still in full control of our civilization, has so little empathy for the person and figure of Jesus. After all, that world still rejects precisely the psychic values that Jesus defends as so crucial in his plea for a humane image of the human being and of God, which for him are non-negotiable.

If two thousand years have not succeeded in ushering in a sweeping transcendence of our exclusively masculine collective consciousness, then is there any hope at all? What is of interest here for our own considerations is that *the psyche itself never ceases to impel the human being to just such a transcendence.* The psyche itself shows us that the blueprint of the humane human being is laid out along lines of a masculine and feminine totality. And the psyche insists on a hearing. But the masculine-centered consciousness, consciously or unconsciously,

is anything but willing to listen. Whether out of a fear of a
loss of prestige, or a thirst for power, or illusions of superiority, or material considerations, that consciousness suppresses the
language of the psyche. And we must by no means forget that
women themselves have always cast their psychic shadows in the
shape of a certain degree of passivity, conservatism, masochism,
and want of a spirit of enterprise, which have only made it all
too easy for men to lord it over them. It would be an equally
lopsided conceptualization, then, to understand women as simple victims of male arbitrariness and lust for power. To be sure,
there have always been individual women in history who have
demonstrated that women, in their own fashion, are basically in
just as favorable a position to cope with reality as are men.

From the model held forth by Jesus, meanwhile, we have
plainly seen that the materialization of a humane model of the
human being will necessarily depend on the interplay of masculine and feminine existential values. Jesus has presented adequate evidence of this in his own person. As for how the psyche
expresses itself to this effect in modern human beings, let us
now rehearse two equally remarkable examples.

A male analysand had the following dream. His dog came
bounding over to him through heavy traffic and tugged him
toward a car. In the car sat his wife. So they were all going
out for a ride. In jumped the dog with a bark, the dreamer
following. It was a beautiful summer's day, and the trio began
their excursion. A little way down the road the dog began to
bark excitedly, as if to warn of some danger. Indeed there had
been an accident, and a disabled vehicle was projecting onto the
roadway on the right. The man's wife, who was driving, had
seen the obstacle, however, and the danger was averted. "Good
that the dog warned us too," she said. After another stretch
of the way they came to a bridge. Slowly and cautiously, the
wife proceeded across the bridge. "After we'd gotten across, we
looked back and saw that the bridge was practically all rotted
away." So all three were happy and relieved to have crossed the
bridge safely, the dog gave a happy yelp, and the car continued
its journey across the lovely summer countryside.

A woman dreamt she was riding in a trolley car, through

a twilight landscape, to reach a large city. Unfortunately the tracks ended some distance from her destination. Meanwhile it had grown completely dark. She could see the bright glow of the city in the distance, but was unable to make out the road that led there. In her predicament she turned to a middle-aged man in work clothes who had also gotten out of the trolley and asked him the way to the city. He replied that she could simply join him, as he was going the same way. Not without a certain feeling of fear and mistrust, she did just that, and off they went. Confidently and surely, the man led the dreamer over the unfamiliar terrain. At last they came to the outskirts of the city, where the man asked her to wait a moment while he stopped into a certain house from which, to her astonishment, he promptly emerged transformed into a fine-looking gentleman. "Excuse me," he explained, "I had to change." Now he was free to lead her to her final destination.

In both of these examples we are struck by the fact that it is the figure symbolizing the opposite sex who assumes the role of leadership, at any rate in the situation at hand. The male dreamer is chauffeured by his wife, the female is guided by the man she meets. Here we have actual illustrations from therapeutic practice of the fact that the human psyche, whether male or female, is always composed of both the masculine and the feminine existential and operational modes, operating in tandem. In the man's dream, the successful outcome of the ride in the car (his life journey) depended on the cooperation of both his instinct (his dog) and his feminine intuition (his wife) in order to overcome the attendant dangers. In the woman's dream, as well, the dreamer cannot make her way alone. The city is ablaze with light (representing self-fulfillment). But the way is dark. The collectivity in which she lives (the trolley car) can carry her a good part of the way. But the last stretch is in the dark and becomes a passage through darkness and uncertainty to an adventure. Here she needs the help of a "man" — that is, her own masculine will to achievement (the work clothes) and spirit of enterprise (her feeling of fear and mistrust, which she succeeds in disregarding). In every psyche then, as we see with particular clarity in these two dreams, masculine and fem-

inine modes of operation are represented, complementing one
another and offering mutual support. The man in the woman's
dream supports her on *her* way to *her* goal, as the woman in
the man's dream sustains him on *his* way to *his* goal. This is
how the mutual completion of which we speak is to be understood. When this complementarity is present, the result is men
and women in their psychic totality, men and women who are
genuinely humane.

Doubtless it is abundantly clear that the pair of dreams we
have just examined are not those of beginners in analysis. They
are mature testimonials to a development that has already taken
place. The respective parts of the dreamers' souls are already
in partnership and collaboration. Let us go back, then, and
examine the beginnings of this humane, totalizing developmental process. A young woman of twenty-eight was not up to the
challenge of breaking out of the cozy, comfortable environment
of her parents' home. Where else, after all, could she "have it
so good"? Thus her personality development was simply stag-
nated. Then she had a dream. She dreamt that her employer's
wife was pregnant and about to deliver. The dreamer was to
assist at the delivery. Unsure of herself, she asked the employer,
the child's father, to help too. But he said he thought no compli-
cations were to be feared. But difficulties there were, and from
the side of the unborn baby, who, it turned out, had a mind of
her own. Speaking from the womb, she declared her refusal to
be born. And despite every effort on the part of the dreamer to
persuade her to the contrary, explaining that she simply must
be born, that this was nature's way, this was the only way she
could survive, the baby only laughed mockingly: "I guess I'm
the one who'd know about that! I'm the one in here, not you!
I won't, I won't, I won't! When you don't want to, you don't
have to. It's nice in here! And I'm just going to stay in here."
And she stuck out her tongue: "Nyahh, nyahh!"

This time we see the beginning of a development. Here
the psychic element of the opposite sex is represented by the
dreamer's employer. The baby's defiant reactions are of course
to be understood as those of the dreamer herself, and represent
the first birth-pangs of personality development. This dream is

almost funny, and could of course lend itself to this interpretation: What a stubborn little girl! And so precocious! She isn't even born yet and she speaks like an orator! If this is a symbol of the dreamer's state of willingness to develop, then we may as well forget the whole thing. But we must not neglect the fact that, in the dream, the dreamer is completely aware of the urgency of the situation. It is a matter of survival. Further analysis must now offer its obstetric capacities. The issue was successful. The patient moved out of her parental home, did well in her exams, and took on responsible employment. But more importantly in the overall connection, she found a partner and could describe this relationship in terms like these: "You get closer, but without giving up a part of yourself. In fact it's just the opposite. You actually discover yourself." A young couple had been started down the path to essential cooperation, to human totality. The refractory suckling, who had been so unwilling to develop, had become a human being who now said: "I'm tired of theorizing. I'm on fire. I want to *do*."

By way of exemplifying the correlative situation, the underdevelopment of the feminine element in the male psyche, let us consider the following case. Despite his extensive development in other areas, a male patient's marriage had remained underdeveloped and primitive in the area of marital intimacy. The first dream he had to report was of a student revolution, in which certain financial considerations seemed to play some role. Our discussion, then, turned on his finances. In this area, I was assured, all was in good order. His wife, a professional accountant, handled their joint income. The analysand himself did not even know how much he earned per month. Now I pricked up my ears! What was it, then, that the students had been revolting against in his dream? Shortly another dream brought the answer. The analysand dreamt he was in an unsegregated public toilet. A young woman made him an indelicate offer, and he disappeared with her into one of the stalls. The analysand showed great embarrassment as he reported his dream. Obviously nothing of the kind had ever taken place in his life. Now, what did the psyche seek to express in this scene in the rest room? Did it mean the analysand's sexual relationship was limited to the area of relief, or one-sided sexual satisfaction? He himself found the intimacies of his marital relationship fully satisfactory. But when I asked what his wife would be likely to answer to this question he seemed startled, and could give no response. And yet they had been married for nine years. So I encouraged him to go ahead and ask his wife the same question. He was shattered by the result. "Honestly," his wife had explained, "I only do it because you want me to."

So this is what his psyche had revolted against in its drastic characterization of his relationship with his wife as an act performed in the rest room. The willing female in the dream represented the current level of his capacity to relate to the feminine. This is how the psyche had decided to appeal to this really very nice, talented young man to raise the level of his intimate life, too, to an authentically humane one. That would mean, from now on, striving to develop his relationship to the other, his approach to a partner, as the genuine address of his feelings. This would be an expression of the feminine existential disposition. The young man had the great advantage of a willingness to implement, immediately and in a sensible way, any suggestion made by the unconscious. Happily, a great deal changed in the area of his marriage, which developed into a genuine partnership.

As we have seen from the foregoing examples, the dream figures symbolizing the masculine and feminine elements of the psyche indicate the degree of development attained by the female or male dreamer respectively. We might say that the psyche is attempting to hold the mirror of self-knowledge up to the dreamer's gaze in the hope that the latter will not only peer into it, but make an effort to reach an even higher level of humaneness. To be sure, the development in question will be subject to a great deal of vacillation.

What implications for his total personality, especially for the feminine element thereof, will be evinced by the following dream, reported by a male student of twenty-four? He was climbing a long flight of stairs, accompanied by a young woman of his acquaintance. As the pair reached the top, it suddenly occurred to the dreamer that he had left his overcoat below. Without a moment's hesitation the young woman hurried back downstairs to bring him his coat, while he simply waited for her. Now we are really back in the present, with the conceptualization of the female as servant or maid in accordance with a male tradition thousands of years old. This young man had a long way to go before he might bring his psyche to the point of constituting a whole person, a humane human being.

Let us look at one last example of the problems involved with the integration of the simultaneously masculine and feminine composition of the psyche. A young woman, single, dreamt she found herself in a room with a great number of other persons. Suddenly there was a commotion. A young man seemed to have gone out of his mind. He was throwing glass arrows in every direction. Those whom the arrows struck tumbled to the floor, some of them dead. Fear seized the dreamer as the young man approached her. To her relief, however, he did not attack her, but merely offered her three of his arrows. The thought occurred to her, "Now I can get even, and go on the offensive." But after a brief moment of reflection she surprised even herself by simply handing him back his arrows with the words, "No, I don't want to kill. And I shan't — you or anyone else." Instantly the man changed and became completely calm. An atmosphere of peace reigned throughout the room.

The aggressive young man with the deadly projectiles of course represents the female dreamer's own aggressive masculine psychic component. Indeed she was an achievement-driven, sharp-tongued, dogmatic person, in her professional as in her private life. With this primitive masculine paraphernalia she foundered, specially in her private life, where she was completely incapable of a relationship. Only in analysis did she recognize that the dangerous man who had frightened her in her dream represented her own self-destructive tendencies. She had to deal with this penchant for assaulting herself. The dream indicated that she had succeeded in doing so. She wanted to kill no longer. Now even the masculine side of her psyche had a better chance of developing. It would or could become her helper in the the process of further progress. An atmosphere of peace reigned throughout the inner psychic process.

Through the use of examples of such diverse types and such different levels of psychic development, we have demonstrated the concrete becoming of what we call the qualification of consciousness. *The essence of this qualification consists in the integration of the masculine and feminine modes of being.* And this integration constitutes the decisive step to the humane human being. Jesus stands as the model of that human being, and we need not indulge in a detailed rehearsal of our considerations to this effect. Psychic spin-offs like dreams attest to the authenticity and actual effectiveness of that model. Men and women come for therapy precisely because their current psychic development falls short of that model. But when they strive after it, when it calls out to them from the depths of their own consciousness, admonishing, demanding, and activating, then there is healing.

The case of the atomic bomb, cited in the opening lines of this section, showed us that it will not in the first instance be the perfection of the psychic functions that will launch the humane human being. Now we have seen that that crucial thrust is the deed of the quality of responsible consciousness. Beck-Gernheim's study provides incontestable proof that all social problems arising in any way from the problem of the sexes have their cause in the masculine proclivity to exclude the feminine, hence once more in a poor quality of consciousness. Any of the problematic aspects of our lives could readily provide us with the premises for the conclusions that we have drawn here. Nor are these dangers, though demonstrated by depth psychology, a mere matter of a one-on-one discussion in the peace and quiet of a therapeutic session. The humanization of humanity, and therefore humanity's very survival, depend on our ability to solve the problems broached here.

Inner Control

The psychotherapist understands Jesus very readily. Jesus is in direct contact with life. He has discovered valid, basic laws of psychic existence. Indeed, he has emphatically installed them at the very center of his speech and activity. That is why we have been able, without contrivance, to adopt elements of that speech and action as governing paradigms for an understanding and treatment of the problems of human beings today. In Jesus and in psychotherapy, then, we see the same, entirely specific, humane image of the human being. Apart from Jesus himself, of course, we as yet possess no concretization of that image.

The most important thing about this humane image of the human being, however, remains to be discussed. When all is said and done, the actual materialization of the humane human being does not depend on coincidences, nor is it subject to manipulation. It is not "makeable" at all, however much we may have spoken of "doing." It rests ultimately on an *in-built drive of the psychic structure of the person* to become all that that person can possibly be. We call this drive the psyche's inner direction or management.

Let us first recall how Jesus speaks of this inner direction, this interior control panel of ours. A universally familiar parable of the gospels, and one central to those gospels, is the parable of the Prodigal (Luke 15:11–32). The younger son violently breaks all ties with his paternal home, demands his patrimony, and goes abroad. He has burned his bridges behind him and evidently intends to assume full responsibility for the achievement of his independence. Surely there can be no objection to his striving for independence. But he goes about it in the wrong way. He cuts himself off from the roots of his existence. He becomes a man without a country, an unstable person at the mercy of life's uncertainties. Thus there is a profound rectitude in his being placed at last among the swine, on a subhuman level of existence. In vain does he seek the help of others, help from without. What wrenches him from his psychic capitulation? The crucial moment has arrived. It will not be what the *Good News Bible* says: that he "came to his senses," that is, that he had become reasonable. Nor was it some sort of "act of contrition," in the spirit of superficial piety. It was something completely different. And here we must take the literal meaning of the text to the hilt. We might render it as follows. "But *going into himself* he said, '...I shall rise and go to my father....'"

Yet the person who returns home is no psychic ruin, regressing to the childhood state of dependence on his parents. No, in his "going into himself," his journey inward, he has seen something quite different. For the first time in his life he has entered into contact with his interior guidance system, in terms of which his father's house now becomes a symbol of his inner capacity for independence. He is no longer the same as when he left home. He has gotten up the courage for self-encounter, the courage to see himself as he really is, as we see from his words to his father on his return. The psychological truth expressed here is that, despite what so many young people think today, genuine independence is not attained in liberating oneself from all external bonds and "going abroad." It is attained in freely following one's inner direction. This interior guidance or management is already there. It may be presupposed. It is subject to *observation* as the self-expression of the psyche. The following cases from actual practice will furnish us with just such empirical evidence.

First, however, let us reemphasize what we have just said about the distinction between becoming independent and simply moving out of the house, lest there be any doubt about it. As the parable itself directly suggests, one can live in one's parents' house and not be independent, but one can also live in one's parents' house as an independent person; likewise one can live elsewhere without being an independent person, or of course as an independent person. The sole deciding factor is whether staying or going is right or wrong in terms of obedience to one's inner guidance system.

This highest inner authority, the control panel responsible for the overall direction or qualification of our humane existence, is also the subject of the passage on the coin of tribute to the Roman Caesar, cited earlier (Matt. 22:15–22). Jesus draws the attention of his hearers from the image of the Emperor on the coin to that supremely interior image stamped on every human being, to heed which is a matter of the highest responsibility. It must be a fact that one can be summoned and addressed by this inner guidance system, since, of all things, even the ill-willed coterie who so confidently expected to entrap Jesus are speechless at his unexpected allusion to it. Not even the

pigheaded can gainsay the reality of the inner steering function
Jesus introduces into the debate.

Likewise to be cited in this connection are the stories of the
pearl of great price and of the treasure hidden in the field (Matt.
13:44–46). As we know, the individual who caught a glimpse of
the precious pearl committed everything he possessed to its ac-
quisition. The farmer who has discovered a large treasure buried
in a field sold everything he owned to be able to buy the field. A
pearl or treasure are symbols of ultimate, binding values. They
correspond to the image of the paternal domicile, or to the image stamped on a coin. They are thrilling symbols, to the point
that they have entered our languages as common expressions.
But more than this, both of these parabolic utterances seek
to indicate that what is at stake with these ultimate values is
the very essence of the humane. Anyone wantonly disregarding
them will forego a magnificent opportunity for living, the highest life capacity of all. Those who have familiarized themselves
with them can actualize them, but only under condition of engaging all of their energies. Then the phenomenon spirals up
and away: the more we actualize these values, the more ready
we become for the engagement they call for. For no longer can
we conjure away this capacity called our inner direction. Now
it is part and parcel of our lives.

But let us see this interior steering faculty at work in some
examples taken from actual practice. A colleague of mine once
recounted to me the following case. For years he had dealt with
a patient who had frightened and shocked both his family and
his therapist with his repeated suicide attempts. But of course
it is impossible to protect people against themselves indefinitely.
After all, they can't just be tied down, and there are suicides
even in institutions. The therapist explained this to his patient,
and discharged him on his own responsibility. Then one day
he received a letter that contained the last dream of his former
patient. The latter had actually executed his intent to com-
mit suicide, but had recalled his analysis and felt compelled to
send his former analyst his last dream. "I was walking through
a military zone. Suddenly my way was blocked by a barbed-
wire fence, with a sign that read: 'Danger! No Entry! Mine

Field!' I didn't care. I jumped the fence." This most unusual
dream demonstrates especially graphically that our inner steering function will not give up till the very end. This patient's
consciousness had long since ceased to be receptive. And yet
his inner psychic control panel was still sending signals, still
attempting to warn him not to leap that fence.

How absurd, in the light of this patient's experience, to saddle the ego with responsibility for everything, when Sigmund
Freud himself refers to the ego as no more than the tiny, projecting tip of a gigantic psychic iceberg.

An elderly married woman decided to go back to school.
Understandably enough, she embarked on her new project only
with great insecurity and diffidence, as it was sure to be full of
challenge and adventure for a person like herself. Her first night
in her new living quarters, she had a dream. "I was standing
alone, at the edge of a pond in a woods. In the middle of the
pond was a lotus blossom — just one. As I gazed at the lotus,
it began to grow. It grew right up out of the lake into my
arms. Instinctively I grasped it by the stem and clutched it to
my breast. Then I perceived a turbulence in the water around
the stem. I waded into the water to see what this disturbance
might mean. To my astonishment, just below the surface of the
water, against the stem of the lotus and apparently attached to
it, I saw a person. I let go the stem and grasped the person.
Pulling with both my arms, I drew her onto dry land. I was
horrified to recognize the inert form of my own daughter. She
opened her eyes. 'Mother,' she said, 'if you hadn't pulled me
out I'd have drowned.'" The woman felt this dream to have
been an endorsement of her new academic endeavors. It was
clear to her now that her plan to resume her studies had been
no arbitrary whim. No, she had actually been following an
inner psychic lead that had been encouraging her to forge ahead
at this transitional time of her life. The dreamer had lived
for many years in the East, where the lotus is a very special
symbol of totality, and this pregnant symbol automatically went
into action in her dream. It grew toward the dreamer, and as
she grasped it, it became a symbol of new becoming: the child
she pulled to shore and rescued. Without this guidance and

encouragement from within, the dreamer felt, she would have lacked the confidence to see her new project through to the end.

Let us have another example, equally meaningful. A woman had a dream about the change of life. "I had died. It was if I were gazing down from the ceiling on my own lifeless corpse. But then I felt an irresistible urge to leave the room. I did so, and found myself somehow wandering above the tops of the trees. Very shortly I noticed that there were others with me, wafting along in the same direction. After some time we all came to a clearing in the woods, and I could see the ground. There below was a hikers' restaurant, where a large number of persons were sitting eating pastry and drinking coffee. I noticed that some of my companions on my journey drifted down to join them. Somehow I was unable to follow. An irresistible urge drove me onward. This happened three times. Each time, more of my companions left me, sinking down and filling the empty chairs. I couldn't understand why I couldn't join them! Somehow I had to keep moving. Suddenly I had a flash of insight. The people down there weren't sitting there because they were having such fun and enjoying themselves so much. They were forced to be there. They had to just sit there. They no longer had any strength inside. And I said to myself, 'That's hell.' I breathed easier. Now I was relieved that I could continue my trip."

This is not a death dream. It is a strikingly typical dream of change and development. Dreams like this often occur in crisis situations. Here the crisis situation was the change of life. The dreamer still felt a great deal of unused energy, and had wondered, at the onset of the change of life, "Is this all there is? Or is there more?" For her there was more. Again we see a kind of inner control panel, or switchboard, what we call our inner direction or management, at work. In this dream it functions as the strength for change.

By way of one last example, let us have a man's dream. "A man was walking up the middle of a road that went up a steep hill. It wasn't easy going. The embankments along the road were bare, but so high that they blocked the man's view of anything around. The strangest thing, however, was that the man had a bag over his head. I ran up to him. 'Hey,' I said, 'take that bag off your head!' 'That doesn't work,' he replied. 'But you can't see where you're going! You'll trip and fall!' 'No,' came the answer, 'that's just it. When I take the bag off I get off the road. Just as long as my inner eye is open!' Completely dumbfounded, I let him plod ahead a while. Then I ran after him again. 'Hey, what's this all about? What are you doing?' 'Getting closer to God,' he said. Meanwhile, I noticed, he had reached the summit of an elevation. We could see the green landscape now, and the road was more level."

The image of the inner eye recalls Jesus' utterance concerning the eye as the inner light that renders all things luminous (Matt. 6:22–23). The description of the terrain suggests a life situation especially difficult for the dreamer. It is most important at such moments to follow one's inner guidance, and the figure in the dream wears a bag over his head to shield himself from any distractions. The frightening, discouraging condition of the road reinforces the symbolism of crisis. "Getting closer to God" doubtless represents coming nearer the desired guiding truth. The dream's ending suggest the rightness of the inner guidance.

Here we have three particularly striking attestations to the truth of what we have been saying about the inner management faculty. We need only observe that the length of the list could be multiplied many times over. I should like to make one point altogether plain, however. In nowise are we dealing with some mystical, preternatural, or otherwise metaphysically mysterious factor. We are strictly within the framework of psychology. Our inner management, represented so clearly in the dreams that we have just presented, belongs to what Jung has called the *self-regulating capacity of the psyche*. This is an enormously important piece of trailblazing on Jung's part, which current psychology is still very far from understanding in its whole scope. Let us add, then, to this last consideration of ours on the subject, the following fundamental observations.

We had set ourselves the task of a reflection on Jesus as a psychotherapist and his corresponding treatment of persons. We showed what it was that, for Jesus, everything depends on: the engagement of the will, the courage for self-encounter, attention to predispositions, and training or exercise. Only the joint operation of all of these, according to Jesus, makes possible the materialization of the *genuinely humane person,* whose base lines we have now endeavored to trace.

This humane human being, this fully human person, is not a conjunction of fragments. He or she emerges completely from within, and thus is constituted in a *psychic totality.* In order to portray this totality, Jesus chooses three particular symbols — the tree, the heart, and the eye, which occur in our dreams today as well and have the same meaning.

Jesus makes a direct and immediate appeal to persons to respond to their potential — to become what they can and ought to be. He has not the least doubt that human beings *can do this if they want to.* This is an established fact for him and forms the basis of his spontaneous, direct grasp of persons that takes us by surprise over and over again.

Only a two-thousand-year dogmatic development has been able to render this crystal-clear picture so exceedingly foreign to us, distorting it beyond recognition. We must endeavor to see through this process of alienation. We must understand it for what it is. It constitutes a phenomenon of *collective projection.* Each and every Christian age has seized the figure of Jesus and overlaid it with its own unconscious wishes and uncritical conceptions. Let us go back to the original Jesus. Today we have the valuable assistance of modern New Testament research to make him visible once more.

When we pay attention to this original or historical Jesus and his treatment of human beings, we are surprised to observe that the basic laws of human existence he has discovered are implemented today as well in the *self-expression of the psyche.* That this is the case, however, can be recognized only by a depth psychology free of doctrinaire prejudices and performing its work independently of the predetermined schemata of any "school."

Further, the point of contact between Jesus' treatment of persons and today's psychotherapeutic effort on behalf of the sick is sunk *deep in objective reality.* Jesus appeals to persons to become what they can and should be. The good offices of psy-

chotherapy likewise reside in the effort to assist human beings
to become what they can and ought to be.

Sigmund Freud locates the ultimate root of any neurosis in
the unconquered oedipus — therefore in the persistence of an infantile disposition. Adler speaks of an entrapment in the quag-
mire of undefeated feelings of organ inferiority. Jung asks what
development problem the patient is seeking to evade. It is not
a renunciation of one's intellectual integrity to pay some heed
to such an evident community of elements. That community, of
course, consists only in the observation that human beings fall ill
when they are not what they should be. My thesis, however, is
that therapeutic success depends on the extent to which the *basic laws of Jesus' model* precisely of a humane human existence
are taken into consideration.

We are not invoking the Jesus model arbitrarily, as an old
schema, or a new one, or as an uncritical subjective presupposi-
tion of our own. We recommend this model because of its own
credentials as *objectively and uniquely correct.* When called to a
humane humanity in the sense that we have expounded, the psyche reacts spontaneously yet today, as we know from experience,
and becomes healthy, as our many examples have evidenced.

In what did Jesus' actual treatment of persons ultimately
consist? Jesus confronts human beings, from start to finish,
with the authentic humane person that *he himself was.* And
thereby he awakens in any person with whom he is dealing the
latter's own capacity for a humanness that will be genuinely humane. This must be the aim of any psychotherapy, in whatever
concrete scientific terms that aim be couched. This is the end
for which we must strive, even if we only strive.

What is astonishing here is that nothing is *done to* the psyche. The psyche is not manipulated, directed, conformed, or
adapted. It is treated, but it is in no way "handled." It is
merely summoned to *unfold and develop responsibly in the freedom of its own self-expression.* This is Jesus' only "method." It
is this that more than anything else brands his approach to human beings as the ideal model for any psychotherapy. And this
is what we mean when we speak of the self-regulating capacity
of the autonomous psyche.[8]

These are the facts before us. Now the practical question arises: Who is a genuine psychotherapist? What can we learn from Jesus' treatment of human beings to help us answer this question?

Chapter 7

Who Is a Genuine Psychotherapist?

Who is actually and properly a psychotherapist? The question has always generated a great deal of controversy, but little consensus, as is openly admitted. Obviously the psychotherapist must be a person of flexibility, broad scientific knowledge, personal integrity, empathy, and so on. But any such catalog of admirable qualities could be lengthened ad infinitum, and we should have an imposing catalog of virtues indeed, but without ever having transgressed the bounds of the relatively self-evident. Nearly all of these personal prerequisites for the practice of psychotherapy would be equally appropriate in a great number of other professions. They are still far from characterizing the specific apparatus of the psychotherapist.

Now that we have acquainted ourselves with so many examples of Jesus' approach to human beings, perhaps we can obtain a basic answer to our question from him. What manner of individual is a genuine therapist? We shall certainly have begun our response basically in accordance with the mind of Jesus if we say: *The therapist must be as flexible as the self-regulating autonomous psyche of the client.*

But let us expand our proposition to make it more precise. What do we mean by flexibility as we find it with Jesus? We shall best answer this question by drawing up a series of theses, expressed in terms of *polarities in a psychic field of tension.*

162

First of all we have the following poles in tension: *uncompromising certitude* and *receptive openness.* Jesus is never the man of the "On the one hand...on the other hand." He takes a position, and demands his fellow human beings do likewise. The parable of the Good Samaritan ends simply and tersely: "Go and do likewise." To the rich youth Jesus says: "Sell everything you have." Martha is reprimanded: "One thing is needful," Jesus tells her. With unsurpassable clarity Jesus expresses his sure conviction: "But I tell you...." He calls all persons to the same uncompromising forthrightness: "Say very simply yes or no. All further words are from the evil one" (Matt. 5:37). But his uncompromising self-assurance is not narrowness, stubbornness, or the rigidity of inflexible principles. Rather it is a firmness and security that is capable of acknowledging the manifold phenomenality of a general principle. To a fundamental decisiveness can correspond a wide-open, honest receptivity. "Whoever is not against us is for us" (Mark 9:40). It is in virtue of this receptive openness that Jesus shatters so many particularisms, especially with his universalization of the notion of "neighbor," and we have seen this in some detail. The evangelist John has captured his spirit of openness when he has Jesus explain, to an ostracized Samaritan woman, that true worship cannot be confined to this particular mountain or that particular temple. "God is spirit," he says, "and those who worship him must do so in spirit and in truth" (John 4:24).

The therapist, too, must manifest an attitude of assurance. This by no means need detract from the objectivity or impartiality of the analytical relationship, as might be objected. Obviously there must be no forcible imposition of the narrow, bounded position of a particular school. This is already excluded by the requirements of the contrary pole of receptive openness. Patients definitely expect the therapist to possess character, to be definite, to be able to take a position so that there can be a discussion. Hesitation and wishy-washiness with respect to one's own position have never accomplished anything. The polarity-in-tension of unequivocal certitude and receptive openness is thus an inalienable prerequisite for a therapist, in order to do justice to the rich multiplicity of the psychic phenomena at hand, and yet at the same time to ensure that the analysis will be the creative collaboration of both parties concerned.

In the second place, we note a psychic tension obtaining in the polarity between an *ability to wait* and *spontaneous intervention*. Jesus knows that psychic development is comparable to organic growth, and that organic growth takes time. Patience, therefore — the ability to wait — is one of the supreme laws of healing. Jesus recounts the paradigm of the seed that grows of itself. The farmer has sown it, but then "he sleeps and gets up, night and day, and the seed sprouts and grows without his knowing it" (Mark 4:26–27). Or again, the winegrower who proposes to have a fig tree cut down because it has borne no fruit for a number of years is admonished to be patient and urged to further endeavors — in a word, to give the tree another chance: "Let it stand this one more year at any rate" (Luke 13:6–9). At the same time, as we have seen in so many different ways, Jesus is past master of the spontaneous intervention. He has an immediate grasp of a situation that demands an immediate decision. "One who puts his hand to the plow and looks back is not the one for the kingdom of God" (Luke 9:62); or, "Let the dead bury their dead. You follow me" (Luke 9:60). He says these things to persons who ought to awaken to the fact that their hour of destiny has sounded.

In psychotherapy, as well, this double mind-set is a basic requirement. Psychic developments can call for the therapist's understanding patience over long periods of time. Or they can clearly appeal to the psychotherapist to rouse the courage for a spontaneous intervention, as a surgeon performs a life-saving operation. We have already seen abundant practical examples of each of the two poles of this dynamic tension.

Third, we have the psychic polarity-in-tension of *engagement* and *distance*. As we have shown, Jesus' feeling is always an engaged feeling. He is touched with compassion for the blind. He is enraged over the profanation of the temple. He scolds the unbelieving cities. He pities those who suffer, and from the bottom of his heart. He sincerely celebrates with bride and groom: he is merry himself and calls on all others to share in his merriment. He rejoices over the sheep that was lost and has been found. But he weeps over Jerusalem. He is mortally afflicted in Gethsemane. On the other hand, Jesus takes us by surprise with his objective distance when basic, essential human values are at stake. He tells of a wedding guest too conceited and self-righteous to don the special robe waiting for him in the vestibule, and who suddenly hears, "Throw him out!" (Matt. 22:1–14). The hard-hearted debtor to whom so much has been condoned now goes to debtors' prison after all (Matt. 18:21–35). And the steward who couldn't think of a thing to do with his one talent loses even that one talent. Perhaps the clearest example of Jesus' objective distance is in the sober realism of the parable of the different kinds of soil.

In psychotherapy the problem is the following. All psychotherapeutic treatment calls for a personal engagement on the part of the therapist. Cold "couch distance" undercuts real psychic development. At the same time, this personal, existential engagement must not escalate into identification, as is so typical of group therapy, for example. This, too, makes development impossible. An exaggerated existential engagement is just as harmful as an exaggerated existential distance, as, once more, we see in Jesus' model.

We could expand our list of polarities. The three we have indicated, however, will suffice to betray the *basic polarity* required in all genuine psychotherapy: *supreme subjectivity* and *supreme objectivity.* Our examination of Jesus' treatment of persons has revealed the last and deepest secret of his effectiveness: he himself, his personality, was his method. And yet, as we have seen with equal transparency, the richness and variety of his personal capacities enabled him to enter upon an existential encounter with persons without ever pressuring or violating those persons in their personality. On the contrary, he convinces persons, he persuades them, he moves them to action, he acknowledges them, he calls them to a genuine partnership with himself in a genuinely humane humanness. There is no mistaking it: he places the burden of the free decision on the personal responsibility of the person with whom he is dealing. It is as if he said to each and every one: "It's all up to you."

If Michael Balint's *The Doctor, His Patient, and the Illness* could cause such a stir in medical circles by pointing up the subjective factor constituted by the physician in medical treatment, it is not difficult to imagine how much greater a role this factor will play in psychotherapy.[1] The first term of our basic polarity, supreme subjectivity, means that the psychotherapist is ultimately his or her own method. Success and healing depend not on the particular school espoused by the psychotherapist, but on how far that psychotherapist has come in the personal actualization of his or her own humane humanness. This will also be the limit to which this therapist's patients can be brought. No analysis outstrips its analyst.

The other term of the basic polarity that must govern the dynamic activity of the psychotherapeutic phenomenon, supreme objectivity, consists in an acknowledgment of the autonomous, self-regulating function of the patient's psyche. The therapist must take full account of this function. Its movement is independent. Only if the therapist is completely willing to allow it to exercise its spontaneous activity will there be any hope of enlisting the psyche as a willing, understanding collaborator and partner. Only under this condition can psychotherapy become what it authentically seeks to be — the joint endeavor of therapist and patient in the achievement of the their supreme common goal, a humanness that is humane in every sense of the word.

Afterword to
the Sixth German Edition

It is a great joy for me to be able to write an afterword to this book, now in its sixth German edition. My special thanks go to Eva Firkel, the Vienna physician and psychotherapist, now deceased, who had such a great reputation both for her scholarly works and for her practice. We never met. Yet she constantly followed my work with special understanding and interest. In her memory, allow me to transcribe a sentence from our correspondence on the present volume. "Whether therapy can succeed or not," Dr. Firkel wrote, "depends on one's readiness to loosen up and unbend. People cemented in 'their way' have no capacity to change a thing" — neither themselves nor their environment, she went on to say.

Predictably, this work has provoked a wide spectrum of reactions. One cannot even begin to respond to the desires of some theologians, whose interest in a study of Jesus in terms of depth psychology is limited to a quest for their own dogmatic theology — all of it, apparently! We are asked where the post-Paschal Christ fits into our investigations, or the doctrine of grace, or indeed the kerygma itself. Questions of that nature betray only one thing: the "cementation" of the inquirers in their categories. Such persons cannot or will not "loosen up and unbend," so as to be able to appreciate any new approaches to a problem. The only thing that can be said to them is that they must learn to. But they are obviously unwilling, at least for the moment. They are afraid depth psychology might poke holes in their theology!

Another group complains that I am too dependent on Jung's

depth psychology. Indeed, some of these objectants voice a droll objection: "There isn't anything in your book that Jung hasn't already said"! Others couch their real intentions in a verdict like: "Rightly understood, and rightly applied, psychotherapy is full of information. It uncovers hidden meanings. It takes what we had discarded as old rubbish and renders it surprisingly current. Seemingly strange actions or symbols can now be interpreted in their reference to the present." Or the author is said to "show the reader the figure of Jesus from a new side. She opens doors to his proclamation that the dogmatists have not discovered. She liberates Jesus from his ecclesial stagnation and places him at our side as the One who heals." Of course, the categories of depth psychology are of help to the author in making her interpretations, runs the gentle postscript.

Other scholars in the field of psychology make precisely the contrary reproach: Why, despite my fondness for certain insights of Carl Jung, do I so stubbornly refuse to acknowledge that I am a psychologist of the Jungian school? I am even pontifically, finger-waggingly admonished that, after all, I ought to know that depth psychology is "only a school"! This dour observation betrays a total absence of the scientific spirit. Here, we may observe with Jaspers, speaks the *Gehäusemensch* — the homebody, all boxed in and unable to peep out over the four walls of a system. Here we have actual professionals in the field of depth psychology answering to Firkel's description of people "cemented in 'their way.'" The essence of their mentality is limitation, and for them the present volume would have been a book with seven seals in any case. We shall never lay hold of the spirit of Jesus with an academic methodology.

Meanwhile, hundreds of letters, not to mention all the discussions I have held in the course of academic gatherings and other large functions, have shown me how fertile an outlook this new approach can provide. Here I have often encountered the reaction that I actually hoped my book would arouse. Catholics and Protestants alike avow: "You have brought Jesus closer to us. You have made him more interesting to us, more relevant to our daily life. We have begun to read the gospels again." The persons speaking or writing in this vein have in many cases

been the "weary and heavily laden." They have been the ones
with the *Leidensdruck,* or burden of suffering, that is indispensable for psychotherapeutic treatment. You might say they are
"the way Jesus wanted them." Jesus never asked his addressees
about their particular dogmatics. He asked them only whether
they were ready to become willing to change. This book is about
that readiness.

Notes

Chapter 1: Jesus the Therapist

1. A word on what we might call the prehistory of our problem: In 1928 minister and psychoanalyst Oskar Pfister insisted, as against Freud, that motifs pointing "beyond any doubt in the direction of analysis" undeniably came to expression in Jesus' thought and behavior, and dubbed these motifs "gleaming footprints" well worth the following. See *Psychoanalyse und Religion,* ed. Eckart Nase and Joachim Scharfenberg (Darmstadt: Wissenschaftliche Buchgesellschaft, 1977), p. 107.

2. Quotations from the Bible have been translated directly from my own translations as they appear in the German edition of this book, where I have not always eschewed faithful paraphrase of the meaning of the original. I have Luther's German Bible constantly at hand as well, together with a modern translation that I particularly appreciate, *Gute Nachricht für Sie,* 2nd ed. (Stuttgart: Bibelanstalt, 1968). English original: *Good News for Modern Man: The New Testament in Today's English Version* (New York: American Bible Society, 1977).

3. Kurt Niederwimmer, "Tiefenpsychologie und Exegese," in *Perspektiven der Pastoraltheologie,* ed. Richard Riess (Göttingen: Vandenhoeck & Ruprecht, 1974), pp. 63ff., esp. p. 69.

4. Ibid., pp. 69–70.

5. Hans-Wolfgang Heidland, "Die Bedeutung der analytischen Psychologie für die Verkündigung der Kirche," in *C. G. Jung und die Theologen,* ed. W. Böhme (Stuttgart: Radius, 1971), p. 51.

6. *Pfarrerblatt,* 78/1:29.

7. Hanna Wolff, *Jesus der Mann: Die Gestalt Jesu in tiefenpsychologischer Sicht,* 3rd ed. (Stuttgart: Radius, 1977).

8. As a scholarly work, the present book takes scrupulous ac-

count of the findings of historical criticism. However, we intentionally present them in language that will be more understandable to a general readership. We also keep these problems in the background; their currency should not constitute a pretext for scholarly discussions that might be of less interest to our readers.

Chapter 2: The Will to Be Well

1. Ernst Bloch, *Atheismus im Christentum: Zur Religion des Exodus und des Reichs* (Frankfurt: Suhrkamp, 1968), p. 42. English translation: *Atheism in Christianity*, trans. J. T. Swann (New York: Herder & Herder, 1972).

2. Rudolf Bultmann, "Das Urchristentum," in *Rowohlts Deutsche Enzyklopädie* (Munich, 1969), 157/8:167.

3. Rudolf Bultmann, *Jesus and the Word*, trans. Louise Pettibone Smith and Erminie Huntress Lantero (New York: Charles Scribner's Sons, 1958), p. 33.

4. For each of the personal case histories recounted in this book I have the written consent to publication of the person concerned. I have further precluded all possibility of identification of the latter by the style in which I have couched these histories.

5. Sigmund Freud, *The Standard Edition of the Complete Psychological Works of Sigmund Freud*, ed. James Strachey (London: Hogarth, 1962), 16:459.

6. Sigmund Freud, *The Future of an Illusion*, ed. James Strachey (Garden City, N.Y.: Anchor Books, Doubleday, 1964).

7. Here we must cite a basic work, completely ignored in Europe: Wilfred Cantwell Smith, *The Meaning and End of Religion: A New Approach to the Religious Traditions of Mankind* (New York: Harper & Row, 1978). See also Otto Wolff, *Anders an Gott Glauben: Die Weltreligionen als Partner des Christentums* (Stuttgart: Kohlhammer, 1969).

8. For the presuppositions of the Freudian school's hopeless battle with religion, generally against the position of that school, although at times in its limited defense, see Eckart Nase and Joachim Scharfenberg, eds., *Psychoanalyse und Religion* (Darmstadt: Wissenschaftliche Buchgesellschaft, 1977).

9. A more detailed presentation, with supporting evidence, is available in Hanna Wolff, *Jesus der Mann: Die Gestalt Jesu in tiefenpsychologischer Sicht*, 3rd ed. (Stuttgart: Radius, 1977), pp. 71ff., 115ff., 164ff.

10. Herbert Braun, *Jesus of Nazareth: The Man and His Time,* trans. Everett R. Kalin (Philadelphia: Fortress, 1979), p. 117.

11. Horst-Klaus Hofmann, *Psychonautik, Stop: Kritik an der "Gruppendynamik" in Kirche und Gemeinde: im Anhang Psychotechnik contra Geist Gottes bei Dietrich Bonhoeffer* (Wuppertal: Aussaat, 1977).

12. Joseph W. Knowles, *Group Counselling* (Philadelphia: Fortress, 1970); Karl-Wilhelm Dahm and Hermann Stenger, eds., *Gruppendynamik in der kirchlichen Praxis: Erfahrungsberichte* (Munich: Kaiser, 1974).

13. Alexander Mitscherlich, "Kekulés Traum," *Zeitschrift Psyche,* no. 9 (1972), pp. 649ff.

14. Wolfgang Kretschmer, writing in *Frankfurter Allgemeine Zeitung* 301/77.

Chapter 3: The Courage for Self-Encounter

1. Jindřich Mánek, *... Und brachte Frucht: Die Gleichnisse Jesu,* trans. from the Czech by Joachim and Ursula Dachsel (Stuttgart: Calver, 1977), p. 114.

2. G. van der Leeuw, *Religion in Essence and Manifestation,* trans. J. E. Turner (Gloucester, Mass.: Peter Smith, 1967), 1:287, 291.

3. Saying no. 283.

4. Lutz Röhrich, *Lexikon der sprichwörtlichen Redensarten* (Freiburg im B., 1974), pp. 748–49.

5. Theodor Reik, *Der eigene und der fremde Gott: Zur Psychoanalyse der religiösen Entwicklung,* foreword to new edition by Alexander Mitscherlich (Frankfurt: Suhrkamp, 1975), pp. 111ff.

Chapter 4: The Prerequisites

1. See Eilert Herms, "Die Funktion der Realitätsauffassung in der Psychologie Freuds," in *Anthropologie als Thema der Theologie,* ed. Hermann Fischer (Göttingen: Vandenhoeck & Ruprecht, 1978), pp. 165ff.

2. See Hanna Wolff, *Jesus der Mann: Die Gestalt Jesu in tiefenpsychologischer Sicht,* 3rd ed. (Stuttgart: Radius, 1977), esp. pp. 75ff.: "Die Frau im zeitgenössischen Judentum" ("Women in Contemporary Judaism"), and pp. 126ff.: "Der kollektive Schatten" ("The Collective Shadow").

174 *Notes to Pages 81–159*

3. Otto Wolff, *Sri Aurobindo: Der Integrale Yoga,* 5th ed. (Hamburg: Rowohlt, 1975), p. 63.

Chapter 5: Getting into Training

1. Kurt Aland, ed., *Synopsis Quattuor Evangeliorum: Locis Parallelis Evangeliorum Apocryphorum et Patrum Adhibitis,* 9th ed., with editoral matter in German, Latin, and English (Stuttgart: Würtembergische Bibelanstalt, 1976), pp. 416, 585. See also Philipp Vielhauer, *Geschichte der urchristlichen Literatur: Einleitung in das Neue Testament, die Apokryphen und die Apostolischen Väter* (Berlin and New York: de Gruyter, 1975), pp. 648–49, 656–57.

2. Herbert Braun, *Jesus of Nazareth: The Man and His Time,* trans. Everett R. Kalin (Philadelphia: Fortress, 1979), p. 168.

3. Ernst Bloch, *Atheismus im Christentum: Zur Religion des Exodus und des Reichs* (Frankfurt: Suhrkamp, 1968), pp. 176, 179. English translation: *Atheism in Christianity,* trans. J. T. Swann (New York: Herder & Herder, 1972).

4. Sigmund Freud, *The Standard Edition of the Complete Psychological Works of Sigmund Freud,* ed. James Strachey (London: Hogarth, 1962), 16:435.

5. C. G. Jung, *Gesammelte Werke* (Olten and Freiburg: Walter, 1971–), 17:195, 197.

Chapter 6: Humane Image of the Human Being

1. Demosthenes Savramis, *Jesus überlebt seine Mörder* (Munich, 1973), pp. 12, 212.

2. Russell Jacoby, *Social Amnesia: A Critique of Conformist Psychology from Adler to Laing* (Boston: Beacon, 1975), p. 105.

3. See J. Illies, *Das Geheimnis des Lebendigen: Leben und Werk des Biologen Adolf Portmann* (Munich, 1976).

4. E. Blechschmidt, *Wie Beginnt das menschliche Leben?* 4th ed. (Stein am Rhein, 1976), esp. pp. 29ff.

5. B. Grzimek, *Auf den Menschen gekommen: Erfahrungen mit Leuten* (Munich, 1974), pp. 376, 516–17.

6. Presented in greater detail in Hanna Wolff, *Jesus der Mann* (Stuttgart: Radius, 1977).

7. Elisabeth Beck-Gernsheim, *Der geschlechtsspezifische Arbeitsmarkt: Zur Ideologie und Realität von Frauenberufen* (Frankfurt: Aspecte, 1976), esp. pp. 6, 10, 154, 164.

8. As the reader will discern at once, chapter 6, "Humane Image of the Human Being," has been especially influenced by Jung's findings, which represent the introduction and earliest validation of the conception of the human psyche as a totality in terms of depth psychology. The new significance of the figure of Jesus for modern times that constitutes the theme of this book has been transmitted to me especially through Jung's conception of the animus and the anima (his pioneer concept of a psychic component corresponding to the opposite sex of the subject, to be integrated into that subject's total psyche), and his demonstration of a centering of the total human being on a psychic midpoint. Despite my deep objective debt to Jung, however, I absolutely refuse to be regarded as a "Jungian." That I represent no school, but go my own way, should be clear from the mere fact that my evaluation and psychological presentation of Jesus has scarcely anything at all in common with Jung's explorations of the problem of Jesus. I should also like to insist, and most emphatically, that the present work is not a theological one. It is dependent on no dogmatic presuppositions whatever. It is an essay in depth psychology, and has no wish to overstep the bounds of its discipline. Indeed it is precisely for this reason that we find the figure of Jesus so arrestingly near.

Chapter 7: Who Is a Genuine Psychotherapist?

1. Michael Balint, *The Doctor, His Patient, and the Illness*, 2nd ed. (Edinburgh: Churchill Livingstone, 1986).

Index of Scriptural References